Running Your Own Restaurant

Running Your Own Restaurant

Second Edition

R. H. Johnson

Hutchinson
London Melbourne Sydney Auckland Johannesburg

Hutchinson & Co. (Publishers) Ltd

An imprint of the Hutchinson Publishing Group

17–21 Conway Street, London W1P 6JD

Hutchinson Group (Australia) Pty Ltd
30–32 Cremorne Street, Richmond South, Victoria 3121
PO Box 151, Broadway, New South Wales 2007

Hutchinson Group (NZ) Ltd
32–34 View Road, PO Box 40–086, Glenfield, Auckland 10

Hutchinson Group (SA) (Pty) Ltd
PO Box 337, Bergvlei 2012, South Africa

First published by Barrie & Jenkins 1976
Second edition published by Hutchinson 1982

Printed in Great Britain by The Anchor Press Ltd
and bound by Wm Brendon & Son Ltd
both of Tiptree, Essex

British Library Cataloguing in Publication Data
Johnson, R. H.
    Running your own restaurant.
    1. Restaurant management
    2. Restaurants, lunchrooms, etc. – Great Britain
    I. Title
    647'.9541'068   TX945

ISBN 0 09 149231 9

Dedication

This book is dedicated to my wife for without her wonderful and constant support and encouragement, I could never have served our trade associations and kindred organisations. Without her it would not have been possible to have succeeded in business, or to have stolen the moments in which to write this book. Respected and liked by customers and staff alike, she is a tower of strength to us all. I can only express the earnest hope that those either engaged or entering this demanding industry of ours are similarly blessed!

R. H. Johnson,
1976.

Contents

Applicant—Staff Records—Legislation that Affects
Staff—Contracts of Employment—Offices, Shops
and Railway Premises Act, 1963—Sanitary Conven-
iences—Dangerous Machines—Inspection—
Wages Regulations—Health and Safety at Work
Act, 1974—Fire Precautions—The Equal Pay
Act—Other Legislation

Foreword

One of the great satisfactions in life is being one's own master, and few enterprises are more adventurous or can be as rewarding as starting one's own restaurant.

This book will, I hope, reduce the hazards of an uncharted shore by providing sufficient aids to sound navigation, or more particularly in this case, to a sound understanding of the nature of running a restaurant.

The main prerequisites for success are a flair for producing well cooked and attractively presented food, an understanding of wine, a willingness to work hard and a liking for people of all types and nationalities. These requirements are not to be regarded lightly for they are essential if your restaurant is to prosper. For those wishing to embark on this friendly profession the chapters of this book will clearly reveal the implications of the tasks they will have to master.

CLIVE DERBY,
Chief Executive,
The British Hotels Restaurants
and Caterers Association

Introduction

The purpose of this little guide to successful restaurant-keeping is to give what I hope will be useful advice and help to those who are contemplating the purchase of their first catering business. It might even be of some assistance to those who have already been engaged for some time in catering and wish to improve their profitability or simply get some ideas. Several years ago when I was a young Commis Chef at London's Waldorf Hotel, the Head Chef said to me 'My boy, you will never finish learning!'. Casimir Dupont was a very wise and experienced man and had been Sous Chef to the great Escoffier at the Carlton in the heyday of the Edwardian period.

Restaurateurs are usually highly individualistic people and while there must obviously be a basic science and know-how, most operators have their own interpretation of the rules. Many get away with it successfully but, in recent years, many have not and the road to Carey Street is littered with broken catering business and dashed hopes. Make no mistake – catering is a science – indeed an art. Success does not come easily. It comes from very hard work, a flair for the trade, sound business acumen and, above all, from 'knowing the ropes' in a practical way. Being a first class chef capable of turning out classical dishes to perfection is all very well and might well result in a full restaurant but if each dish is being sold at cost it will not mean a happy bank manager. Being a top-flight interior decorator and designing a beautiful restaurant is absolutely no good if the food is badly cooked and the service slow. Because one's wife is a good cook is not really a good enough foundation for thinking 'Let's open a restaurant'. However, we all have to start somewhere.

In recent years the amount of legislation churned out through the State 'sausage machine' by successive governments has all added to the difficulties and pitfalls. To those of us who have grown (groan would be more apt) with all the more recent laws, it is bad enough but at least we have been able to adapt ourselves. To the newcomer it can be rather daunting to say the least. If then these few opening remarks have not now succeeded in frightening you sufficiently to think of an easier way of earning a living and making your first million, then I hope that the next 200 pages or so will help you on the way. I do not think that there can be a tougher industry to work in. It is also the most fascinating and soul-satisfying. Welcome to the Club.

R.H.J.

CHAPTER 1

First Considerations

Diversity

There are few industries which are as diverse as catering. Apart from chain-operated eating houses where menus are based on a common company policy, very few restaurants or cafés are the same as each other. Such differences are due to a multiplicity of reasons. Among the foremost of these is often the experience and expertise of the proprietor or proprietress. It is indeed a wise man who knows his limitations! It would be foolish to be pretentious. We all know the type of establishment we would like to operate but have we either the capital or the necessary ability? Remember that we are thinking in terms of the small business operation.

Staff

The industry is desperately short of skilled workers despite the efforts of our Training Board and of all the technical colleges. It would be unwise to stake 'your all' in the first instance in any kind of enterprise where you are going to be totally dependant on your staff. You should be sufficiently skilled so as to be able to step into the breach in any part of the business at any time and, perhaps even more to the point, to start off in a key role. In my restaurant I used to employ some forty staff, both full and part time, and additional to exercising constant super-

1

vision, my wife and I often had to 'step in'. Had we not been prepared to do this, and able to, the result would have been the difference between happy and satisfied clients and very disgruntled ones. An establishment which is totally reliant on its chef or cook often has a constant variation in standards as they come and go, and even complete stoppage if they are sick or walk out in a fit of pique. If we recognise this need to be a little self-sufficient as a first practical step, then this will assist in the important decision of the type of place to buy. How big? How simple or complicated? What particular slice of the market are we aiming at and, above all, how much can we afford.

Position

Where is the business going to be situated? Is it to be an existing business or are we going to adapt premises (if allowed) and start from scratch? Is the trade going to be purely seasonal or is the trade all-year-round? Is the selected business in an area which will support evening trade if it does not already do so? If so, then what kind? It may be near a theatre or cinema, a railway station or a beauty spot. It may even be out in the wilds. Is it a working-class district, suburbia or in the stockbroker belt? Is there potential for trade development and in what direction? Why is the business for sale? There may be a very good and valid reason but there could equally be an obscure one known only to the vendor. What type of trade exists? It is not easy to change a style of trade easily. A bad name tends to stick but, in any case, the new owners will have to lose the old trade and woo the new. If buying an existing business, how long have the present owners been operating? Have the accounts been properly kept and audited and what kind of profit margins have resulted? What has the trading trend been during the past three years? Allowing for inflation, has the trend been up, down, or even static? Other important considerations come to mind. What is the state of the decoration, the age and condition of the essential equipment which might well involve immediate capitalisation – even the state of the roof if it is a fully repairing lease. These then are just some of the first considerations. But let us go back to the beginning.

Feasibility

In these days of high-pressure commercialism, one often hears the phrase 'feasibility study'. Really all it means is 'using your loaf'! To be fair, however, there is a bit more to it than that or you would not be reading this book. The usual tendency when starting up for the first time is to buy an existing business and try and carry it on, gradually introducing some innovation. There is, of course, nothing wrong with this. There can even be some advantages perhaps. It can provide some guidelines. It also means too that there is trade there and can be a lot easier than starting from scratch as I did. Let us examine the pros and cons.

Scope

There are many reputable agents specialising in the sale of cafés and restaurants through the media of the trade press and other journals. Because of the diversity of the industry, there is usually a very wide range of businesses for sale in all sorts of localities. Most will claim some special attribute – enormous profits, scope for increased trade, immaculate condition, etc. One wonders often why they are selling: but sometimes, of course, the reason is genuine. Retirement or ill health are often reasons in the case of small businesses. Some will offer the freehold, some a lease. Whatever the reason however, it should be treated with great caution and the purchase regarded with complete detachment after examining all the facts that can be marshalled.

The choice can be bewildering but this first step of selection is vital. At this stage the available capital is paramount, always remembering that reserves are important. Sometimes a loan is offered by the agents or even the vendor. Certainly no undertaking of this sort should be entered into without the advice of a competent accountant who will be able to assess the interest rates and the ability of the business to sustain payment. Coupled with this however must be your own ability to operate successfully the chosen business. This is important. There may be a competent staff but there is no guarantee that they will stay after you have taken over. Some of my staff had been with me twelve, fifteen and nineteen years but once, when an unfounded rumour started to circulate the City that we were selling, quite a few of them wanted to give notice. We had to insert an advertisement in the local press to dispel the rumour. The present owners might be working a twelve-hour day, seven-day week and nearly killing themselves – hence perhaps a high turnover figure. You may not want to do this!

Armed then with this kind of thinking, we can now take an objective view of the market. You will, or should, have some preconceived ideas of the kind of business and the degree of commitment you are prepared to take on, and indeed the area of the country that you favour. A look through the agents' lists or the commercial columns of the trade press should now give you some sort of selection. Like buying a house, you will undoubtedly finish up with a compromise after many disappointments with the ideal business having just been sold in front of you.

Viewing

Reference has already been made, in passing, to some of the points that must be thought of. Let us now assume that an appointment has been made to view the property. Before you actually meet the vendors you should carefully weigh up the district and the type of trade which will be attracted. Take note of the trading position and the outside appearance. Car parking is vitally important in many cases these days. If the establishment is not lucky enough to possess one of its own, what are the local facilities like? To be surrounded with double yellow lines with the nearest public car park some hundreds of yards away will not attract the motoring public who are notoriously lazy. If the possibilities are only for a heavy luncheon trade in a busy city centre and catering for mainly office workers, then car parking obviously does not matter. If, however, you have ideas and ambitions for a good class licensed evening trade, then it well could. If the exterior is not prepossessing and, because of design and surroundings could not even respond after decoration, it might not attract the class of trade you have in mind. However, more of that anon. If possible, have a look at the trade being done at what should be a peak time without disclosing your interest. This should tell its own story, although not necessarily – we all get the odd slack period. What local competition did you notice on the way in?

First impressions

Attention should be paid to the first impression, for this is always important. If you like it then there is a good chance your customers will too, bearing in mind the type you will wish to cater for. Are the furnishings and fixtures and fittings of good quality or likely to require immediate replacement? These can be very costly items should this be the case. The state of internal decorations should also be noted. How are the staff dressed and what is their attitude? Is it friendly and welcoming, or cold and disinterested? A careful note of the style of menu being offered and particularly of price structure should be made. The poor chap may be under-selling and for the new owners to correct this would result in immediate loss of trade. To this you might say good riddance!, but it all has to be rebuilt. The books should reveal the true position, however, when we come to them.

Profitability

It is difficult, when dealing generally with a hypothetical sale, to have fixed ideas in terms of profit margins. I do not believe that the small businessman looks at things such as return on capital investment, in anything like the same way as a large company would with a chain of managed houses. To him his business is his living and is quite dependent on his own degree of effort. Very often he has all his savings invested in it. It is his home, his life and his hobby all rolled into one. Once we start to come into the higher-priced market involving many thousands of capital investment, then of course a totally different standpoint emerges. We are not concerned in this book with this aspect of finance. It would be pointless and out of context.

These remarks are not intended to suggest for a moment that the small restaurateur should be any the less professional or should not concern himself with the efficient running and profitability any less than his big brothers. It is simply a different approach with a different set of priorities permitting an individual style of operation. Profit margins will vary considerably depending on many differing factors which will be discussed in the relevant chapter. Obviously, depending on the amount of the purchase price and whether it is freehold or leasehold, long or short term, one has a right to expect a commensurate return. It would be fair to say at this stage that one could well find a very much higher percentage of profit from a business selling high profit lines on a very quick turnover in low-rated premises which did not cost more than a fraction of another doing a slow trade of a much higher class – the overheads of the latter being considerably more and eating into the gross profits. The former, 'bashing it out' and turning over his seating every thirty minutes, could well make a lot more money, and could well have paid much less for his premises!

Spending Power

It is important that you ask to see audited accounts and balance sheets going back at least three years. Remember that any turnover figure will doubtless include Value Added Tax. This should be immediately deducted and disregarded, since it belongs to the government. It is a useful guide when going round businesses to divide turnover by the number of seats to see what the seating capacity earns. Very few restaurateurs will be able to tell you how many 'covers' or main meals they have served in a given period with any degree of accuracy. To me 'spending power', the average spending per customer/head, is one of the most important statistics I keep. Together with this the exact number of customers served is a known fact. With this knowledge one can see at a glance the progress the business is making in real terms. Try your 'vendor' out but do not be disappointed if he cannot tell you; not many can.

Overheads

You will naturally wish to know details of all overhead expenditure and these will be contained and detailed in the statement of accounts if they have been properly summarised. The percentage of wage cost will vary considerably from establishment to establishment depending on the kind of trade done and whether, because of this, it has to employ skilled craftsmen or semi-skilled labour, or perhaps waitress or counter service. Naturally the amount of rent, if leased, and the cost of the rates will need to be known and assessed; also fuel, light and power charges, laundry, stationery and telephone, maintenance to plant and machinery. All these costs and many more should be separately annotated. The percentage of gross profit should be clearly shown and the final net taxable profit. The balance sheet as opposed to the profit and loss account, in which we are interested, will be more of a personal statement of the vendors assets, etc.

Professional Advice

Whilst it should be possible for the prospective purchaser to gain a good insight from the accounts of the prosperity of the business it would, in any case, be wise to get an accountant to cast his professional eye over things. If you do not have an accountant already, you are going to need one sooner or later, so why not get one now. You should preferably go to one who specialises in small businesses. Ask around your friends, even your bank manager or solicitor, but do find a reputable firm to handle your affairs. You cannot possibly operate without a good accountant these days. The tax man does not always know his way around some of the more involved legislation of recent years, so how can you hope to on your own.

Layout Facilities

Assuming that from the books you are satisfied that the business is genuine and that the reasons for sale are not too hard to believe, let us move out of the office (or front parlour) and have another look around. The kitchen is where it all happens so we will start there. Another chapter will deal with this important subject so perhaps just a look will do at this stage. On the type of business you are buying will depend the shape, size, workability and equipment factors. All we are interested in are a few salient points. First, is the kitchen and preparation area on the same level as the main dining area? If not, then how is service affected? By lift (or by stairs perhaps)? Heaven forbid! The disadvantages of a kitchen on a different level are legion. It slows service, makes communications difficult, food gets cold and, if the lift is hand-operated, adds to the work load. On top of this, regulations now require a certificate of annual inspection and maintenance. If it is an electrically operated lift then you can bet your last halfpenny it will break down on a Saturday night! Please do try and keep away from this sort of situation. The drawbacks of a kitchen on another floor are considerable. The main kitchen should be on the same level and most advertisements will boast of this fact. As far as I am concerned, it is a 'must'. A preparation room, larder or bakery is a different matter since they are not so involved with service speed and convenience.

Equipment

The equipment should, as far as possible, be of commercial heavy-duty design and of stainless steel. It should be well laid out in a workmanlike way to permit free movement. Ventilation is very important for, quite apart from working comfort, the restaurant should be free of cooking smells. Proper canopies with extraction should be evident. Ideally the floors and walls should be tiled, and work benches not of wood. The kitchen should be well lit. Have a look at the quality of the pots and pans. Will they all want replacing? How much refrigeration is there and how old is it? Has all the equipment been kept on a regular maintenance schedule agreement? What subsidiary equipment is there? Food mixers, electric slicer, potato preparation, etc. Are there proper pot-washing facilities and storage?

One of the most important functions to be performed is that of dishwashing – one stone sink is not good enough. Is there a modern dishwashing machine installed and where, in relationship to the restaurant, is it? What is its capacity/performance factor relative to the business being done, and to what you hope it will be?

How is the service effected from the hotplate? Is the 'flow' properly thought out and is there sufficient hotplate capacity? Is there 'bain-marie' storage for soups, etc.?

Utility Supply

To conclude this quick appraisal, what method of hot water supply is there? A system that runs cold after a few minutes is not much use when you are busy. A few questions regarding electricity supply might be pertinent. Is it single phase or three phase? When was it last rewired and what is the present loading capacity – in case you want to move in some more heavy-duty electric equipment. At the same time it might be worth asking what size gas supply there is to the kitchen.

Staff Room

The staff require separate changing rooms and toilet facilities in certain conditions (see Chapter 12). Enquire whether these are provided or not and also if lockers are supplied for them depending on the number employed.

Stores

Have a look at the storage facilities for dry goods, liquor, and greengrocery. There should be ample and secure storage for both liquor and dry goods. Greengrocery should be in a separate cool and dry place but near to the kitchen. Next take a look at facilities for beverage making – tea, coffee, etc., and type of equipment in use. A new café set can be expensive.

The Restaurant

After another inspection of the restaurant dining room, you can then go off and do a few sums with your new-found accountant – and possibly also with that friendly bank manager, before a final decision. Few restaurant dining rooms are alike, except possibly the period type where beams, white walls and ladder-back or wheel-back chairs seem to be the common form. It is not proposed to discuss design at this juncture; all we are concerned with is the general ambience and appointments, toilet facilities, number of seats and flexibility of arrangment and general condition of furnishings. Is the layout attractive to the eye and the first impression good? Is it warm and welcoming in general atmosphere – the sort of place where new customers will say at once 'This is nice!'? Take note of the lighting arrangements and consider whether you will wish to change them.

Depending on the style of business, what are the finishes on the tabling? Formica, polished wood, baize-covered, glass-topped or whatever? They should be practical for their purpose and, whilst not so large as to waste valuable space (which has to earn money), comfortable to sit at. The chairs or banquette seating should be similarly considered. What kind of cash register is being used? Is it modern, multi-total if licensed, well-maintained, or, perhaps, even rented?

If the room is carpeted, have a look at the wear and tear. Is there good cleaning equipment? Perhaps it has a polished wood floor or even thermoplastic tiles. Either way, note the condition. Finally, what wall coverings are there? Ideally they should be 'long-term' finishes that require a minimum of re-decoration. Remember that every single item which will require early replacement, renewal or redecoration is going to eat into your starting capital. Prices being what they are now, you could be in for a nasty shock if you have to re-equip to a large degree and you might easily overextend yourself. In any case you must have some capital reserves for contingencies.

Leasehold

The question of the terms of the lease must be carefully gone into. Is it inside repairing only or fully repairing? If the latter, remember that this includes the roof. In this case a general survey would be advisable, and make sure all the 'dilapidations' have been settled between the outgoing tenant and the landlord and that your own position is fully agreed and protected. The length of the lease will, of course, be of particular interest: If a long term remains there will not be much to worry about as the rent is bound to be favourable. If however only a short period is left it is imperative that the future prospects and rents are fully known and if possible a new lease negotiated before signing any binding contracts for the purchase of the business. Rent 'reviews' can be frightening.

Freehold

If purchasing the freehold then any competent solicitor will, of course, carry out all the necessary searches. Many businesses have in recent years lost half their trade, and more even, after a new motor road has cut them off from the other side of the carriageway or a new development has taken place. The fullest enquiries should be made, both officially and even unofficially in the local pub.

Take-over Date

On the assumption that you and your professional advisers are satisfied that it is safe to proceed, the usual form of completion through your solicitors can be effected and a take-over date agreed. Some thought should be given to this of course, particularly if it should be a purely seasonal business. The long cold winter months might lie ahead with nothing much coming in. On the other hand, and assuming you can afford it, it might be an ideal opportunity to refurbish, change the style and re-open in the spring with a new image!

Change of Use

So far the question of buying an existing business has been dealt with. It is, of course, possible to start from scratch. In which case permission for 'change of use' will have to be given by the local authority under the Town and Country Planning Act, 1971 before there is any question of proceeding further. Without this consent, which might involve being re-rated in any case, it will not be possible to set up and commence trading. The following pages of this book will, it is hoped, give you all the necessary know-how to operate your own newly founded enterprise. It would not, in the ordinary way recommend starting from scratch to any but an experienced caterer because I believe that a start in this way calls for much more expertise and flair. You can, however, completely dictate the style of operation from the word 'go'. It could grow quickly if in the right trading position and in experienced hands.

CHAPTER 2

Locality and Feasibility

Site Selection

In briefly dealing with selection of type, size and location of the projected business in Chapter 1, a glimpse of the problems involved will have been obtained.

Differing points of view regarding trading position are sometimes expressed. I do not personally believe that 'position' is everything. One finds quite excellent and exceptional restaurants in the most unlikely places and they may well have a quaint kind of attraction because of this. Whatever theory is put forward there is usually a circumstance to disprove it. However, it would be very fair comment indeed to say that such establishments usually show exceptional flair and are operated by expert restaurateurs of very wide experience. Such eating houses are discovered by the public and their reputations spread like the ripples in a pool – not because of a conscious marketing policy, but by word of mouth passed from friend to friend. These then are the exception rather than the rule. What are the rules then of site selection?

We have already noted the quite extraordinary diversity of operations. Cafés of all kinds, restaurants of all types, franchise-operated speciality houses – you name it! Broadly speaking it is almost entirely a question of meeting a consumer need in a particular area. The particular success of any one specific business should be disregarded at this stage. It is quite possible, and indeed sometimes the case, to find two or three restaurants quite close to each other and of similar type, but one is always full and the others empty. If the successful proprietor took over his less busy neighbour the chances are that he would fill that restaurant too. Not then so much a question of the consumer need being saturated, but more of management flair on the one hand, and lack of it on the other! To succeed, however, a 'fast food' type of operation would have to be sited in a High Street. Since we can only be theoretical, however, it will be necessary to stick to the normal guide-lines.

Consumer Need

If one is going to start a restaurant or café from scratch, and it is really to those that this chapter mainly applies, the need to research into consumer need is, of course, paramount. Forgetting the exceptions which were referred to at the beginning of this chapter, it would not be sensible to set up a high-class establishment in what might be a basically poor area. Whilst a good restaurant will draw its motoring clientele from quite a wide surrounding area, a business usually trades in a built-up area from its immediate local population, certainly as far as its regular trade is concerned. Conversely, of course, it is not feasible to set up a working-class café in the middle of the stockbroker belt. A very careful survey of the projected area and its attendant possibilities is a necessity. Due regard should also be given to any particular local attractions or amenities, and when these are likely to provide the source of business. Are they the sort of thing which will stimulate evening trade, Sunday trade or perhaps only a heavy lunch trade for example? Such amenities, if they are to be seriously considered as an influence, should be of a regular nature and not just something which will mean one week's peak trading once a year such as, say, a county show.

Where no present business exists near, for example, a complex of office blocks, there might well be a wonderful opportunity to open a sandwich bar with take-away trade in mind. A similar trading position could well offer excellent scope for a cheap, simple and fast lunch trade, but be prepared

to accept Luncheon Vouchers in plenty. In this particular
trading area a specific kind of market exists, i.e. office workers.
If they eat lunch they will require something quick and reasonably satisfying but not too expensive. Probably being, in the
main, young ladies, they may well be diet and figure conscious.
This might encourage you to feel that there could well be an
opening for a 'salad bowl' or 'weight watchers' type of business. Whilst some major companies might offer their employees
canteen facilities with subsidised meals, not all do by any
means. However, it would be worth making a few enquiries
before you take the plunge, or it may be a few months of
wondering why you are doing so little business before you
discover the reason. A sandwich bar expertly and imaginatively run is a high-profit earner over short hours, and this
type of operation often does very well where there is a large
office community. Whilst this kind of 'office' trade tends to
centre round a peak of a two-hour lunch period, it could
possibly be coupled with evening trade if there was perhaps a
theatre or cinema or two nearby. There is an additional advantage that in such an area there is a tendency for evening car
parking to be easier once the office workers have gone home.
It obviously depends on the area.

Trading Hours

A word or two here about the question of meal times and
opening hours might well be considered before going further,
because this particular question is very pertinent to the issue
of 'What kind of trade are we going to do?'. Looking back I
am in little doubt that the decision I took many years ago to
ignore traditional meal times was right in our own case. My
own thoughts were quite simply these. The premises are open
from 10.00 a.m. until 10.00 p.m., the staff are here, the place is
heated and lit so when my competitors say at 2.00 p.m. 'Sorry,
too late for lunch,' I shall be waiting with my arms open. The
consequences have been very successful and the restaurant
kept busy with people such as 'reps', publicans and others who
work habitually through the normal lunch period, eating in
the afternoon. The trading situation in my particular ancient
city made this possible. It might not happen everywhere of

course. We were fortunate that we carried on quite a substantial trade for a full twelve hours continuously thus ensuring a very high cashflow-per-seat factor. It is also worth mentioning that we are not in the 'High Street' trading position. But I am not trying to sell my business here; I merely quote it as an example to debunk the idea that lunch must be served from 12.00 until 2.00 p.m., tea from 4.00 until 6.00 p.m. and dinner from 7.00 until 9.00 p.m. You might well say 'Surely you needed to rest sometime!' – and of course we did. It is all a question of organisation, but more of that later.

The opening, or trading hours, are affected both by the kind of business done and the location. The reverse, of course, is just as true. These two factors are completely interrelated. Let us consider the case of a business situated in an early morning market such as Covent Garden, Smithfield or Billingsgate. The type of clientele will require a somewhat down-to-earth style of catering and, of course, operating in the small hours principally – even all night. They are, in the main, heavy manual workers and will therefore require the kind of food to match their physical demands. You might call it perhaps 'rough and ready' but such customers expect a good, clean and honest standard. Therefore furniture, fixtures and fittings must be consistent with requirement and practical for their purpose.

Transport Cafés

The same remarks concerning 'appointments' apply in strong measure to a transport café but the hours of operation again are somewhat different. Long-distance transport operates over a twenty-four hour period. The drivers have a tedious demanding job requiring considerable concentration, particularly with TIR vehicles sometimes driving right across Europe. The law requires rest periods for them. They are quite discerning very often and, perhaps even more than our 'market porters', can be quite critical of poor food, service and surroundings. A 'report' of a poor cup of tea can travel up the motorways very quickly and many a reputation has been lost or ruined on this particular commodity alone. Since the build up of TIR traffic from the Continent, large numbers of continental drivers now make their way from the Channel ports to all parts of the country. You may have seen the *Les Routiers* plaque exhibited outside transport cafés around the country. This organisation, which exists to recommend good clean cafés, has done much to raise standards in France and elsewhere on the continent. It is rapidly gaining ground in the United Kingdom.

However, since the building of new motorways, it is much more difficult to operate a transport café privately in the way we used to know them, as the motorway service area operated by the big companies under government licence have taken over much of the trade. There are, of course, still quite a number of the older establishments still operating on the old routes such as the A1 although some of these have seen their business halved by the introduction of a dual carriageway. Unless in a remote area, it would prove difficult, I think, to obtain planning permission to open a new business. The current cost of land and the necessity to provide a really large car park and proper access would make its costs prohibitive in any case. Quite often, too, in the true transport café, overnight sleeping accommodation in dormitories is a need which should be met. It is, however, quite possible to offer much simpler facilities and many do. They can be a very sound and prosperous type of business to acquire and not requiring too great a degree of culinary expertise. Remember that good 'cuppa' though, or you will never make the grade with the 'knights of the road'!

Tea Rooms

Probably one of the easiest conversions from 'home' to 'small business' is perhaps to start the typical 'Ye Olde Tea Shoppe'. These abound in most country villages and many a reader has, I am sure, partaken of scones, butter and jam and a home-made cake eaten off willow pattern plates and washed down with good British tea. Almost an institution in fact. In summertime they can be quite busy little places but usually tend, by their very nature, to be seasonal. It is perhaps doubtful if you would ever make your fortune, but certainly such kinds of small business, when properly conducted, provide a comfortable living and a pleasant way of life in one's home. Staffing requirements are usually comparatively light, such tea rooms being ideally suited to being run by a lady with one or two part-time staff. Equipment needs too are fairly simple when compared with the traditional restaurant. This means that capital costs can be kept low.

Depending on the size of the house or cottage, it would probably not be necessary to proceed with much structural alteration. It is surprising how even a normal-sized dining room or parlour can be made to accommodate a couple of dozen people when imaginatively planned and thought out. The area most likely to require attention would be the kitchen as, almost certainly, additional preparation and baking capacity would have to be provided. This would obviously depend on the simplicity or otherwise of the food and beverages to be sold. Depending on the degree of bureaucracy exercised by the local planning authority, it should not prove too difficult to obtain permission for 'change of use'. Such authorities, however, are very critical sometimes of parking facilities and particularly if the business will be situated on a busy main road. If there are already double yellow lines in existence and no parking facilities, I should not bother further. There are, however, other forms of trade other than the motorist such as hikers, ramblers and even cyclists. You might even be near a pony-trekking trail. Remember what we have said about 'consumer need'. It would be pointless to open a modest tea room even, if there was no trade there to support it and only the birds would profit from the stale scones! Trading hours would cover morning coffee and afternoon teas principally, unless of course a light snack lunch trade was also envisaged.

Class of Trade

So far we have looked at four specific examples of the catering trade. All of them cater for a particular and differing type of client with a different consumer requirement. The young female office worker would feel rather conspicuous and out of place in the market situation and in any case the hours of trading are not right. The 'strawberry tea' would not be right for transport drivers for I doubt if the tiny scones would be substantial enough! In any case the tea room would not operate all night when our 'knights of the road' tether their steel chargers outside and the needs of the inner man are paramount. Either the trading hours are not suitable and the environment wrong, or the type of fare is not consistent with the needs of the client. This then is really what it is all about. Suiting the business to the local needs and the demands of the particular type of client that is expected to patronise the business.

With the more traditional kind of restaurant operating throughout the day, the hours of trading can be more flexible since the general public from all walks of life are the customers. The type of client which is attracted is more often than not dictated by the character of the restaurant itself, the kind of menu offered, the hours it chooses to operate, whether it is licensed, and above all the price range. If one is starting from scratch it is possible to influence from the word 'go' the particular type of client and 'following' that one would like to have. This can be effected by the kind of ambience, décor and appointments that are provided, and the class of menu and price structure. Whilst the spread of money is more evenly distributed than it used to be, people are still, to a large extent, class conscious, and feel ill-at-ease and uncomfortable in an environment to which they are not ordinarily used.

It would be fair comment to say, in passing, that the large companies through the medium of their speciality eating houses such as Texas Pancakes, Golden Egg, Wimpy and franchised outlets have introduced a 'classless' type of clientele. Since, however, a large percentage of these operations are either in London's West End or major city centres, it means that they are able to cater for a very considerable 'passing trade' drawn from a wide public. Their success is owed to considerable market research, experience and capital resources. Many of these operations are franchised by national and multi-national companies through their subsidiaries, and this aspect and the advantages of 'going franchise' will be enlarged on later. The possibilities are viable and interesting to the aspiring caterer. However, there is still plenty of scope for the small restaurateur or café proprietor to plough his own furrow and develop his own business based on his own individuality.

The 'Trading 'Mix' '

What is your idea of your own favourite restaurant? The difficulties of running the kind that you would like to, and actually achieving it, have been recognised in Chapter 1. In my experience of life, most things end in a compromise – doing the best you can with an opportunity, with the resources that you have available, and with the expertise that you have at your fingertips. Somewhere along the line is the right 'mix'. If you are able to open a completely new establishment then presumably (and hopefully) you will first have done your sums correctly. You will have carried out a market feasibility study – in other words you will have ensured that the potential is there for developing your business and that the chosen area will provide sufficient trade of the type you want. You will have costed the operation carefully and satisfied yourself that your cash resources provide sufficient reserves to equip and furnish satisfactorily and still leave enough to provide the necessary 'cushion' to carry you through the first year of operation. Assuming that all the foregoing essential factors are observed, there remains the question 'What kind of trade?'.

If you are an experienced chef with top-grade experience, then a classical menu is probably well within your accomplishment. Your particular ideal then might be a French restaurant with menu and wines to match. There is, of course, a constant market for this particular type of business. It is, however, a fairly narrow market and, of course, specialised. By its nature it is expensive in raw materials and, by virtue of its need of expertise, costly in labour. It is the kind of restaurant where people do not eat of necessity but where they choose to entertain or celebrate. In consequence, unless very well established in a fashionable area, trade tends to patchiness and trading hours are late evening.

If you intend to be more or less single-handed in the kitchen to begin with, remember that probably you alone will be capable of producing the menu and will be chained to the kitchen stove. If you become sick, or have an accident, what happens to the business if you are the only one capable of the work? The difficulties of obtaining technically qualified staff have to be recognised these days unfortunately. Often a good solution is to try and liaise with the local catering technical college and staff the business gradually with youngsters who have obtained their City & Guilds craft certificates. The same would apply to staffing the restaurant on the service side as a 'silver service' style of operation would be expected in this kind of establishment. Whilst décor is usually expected to be plushy, I do not necessarily hold with this point of view. I know of one particular Swiss restaurant more than 150 miles from London where the dining tables are of scrubbed wood, the food excellent and the reputation very high.

Trading Policy

I believe very firmly that, as I have written elsewhere, 'position' is not everything. If you really give the public what they want in terms of good food, friendly service and reasonable comfort (in that order), then they will find you, stay with you and tell their friends. Nothing pays in business in the long term like an honest trading policy. The fact that some restaurants are always busy and are successful whilst their neighbours are bereft of customers is not accidental. It is, in simple terms, that the customer is being well looked after, the food good and the price structure competitive – in short, value for money. This applies more particularly in the 'popular' sector of the trade. It is also a mistake to be pretentious and to try to offer dishes which are poor imitations of their classical forebears. It is almost fraudulent!

It is not really the purpose of this book to write many words about what are purely exotic restaurants – Chinese, Indian or the like. They are very individualistic and something of a mystery to the author. Whatever the style of the establishment, however, many of the comments relating to our more traditional British restaurants must be just as pertinent; a survey of the area and its potential, for example. One unfortunate case occurred not far from where I live a year or so ago: two premises, one an existing café and the shop next door, came on the market together. They were both bought by Indians separately and without the other's knowledge. They opened weeks later as Indian restaurants! What is more, there was already one such restaurant functioning in a neighbouring street. This just shows what can happen, and is termed 'market saturation'. However, there is obviously a point where someone suffers and the little story just recounted shows how careful you have to be.

Franchising

There has been tremendous growth in the past few years in the franchised 'fast food' operation. This system of trading is an excellent way of breaking into the business without necessarily having any experience of it. It can even represent a form of investment by starting a chain of such operations with all of them under management. The staffing of them does not even require skilled personnel in many cases. Several of our national and multi-national companies offer restaurant franchises through their widely-known and well-publicised subsidiaries. There is now, however, an increasing tendency for some of them to run such establishments themselves, under management, thus increasing their viability. Franchise terms and facilities offered by companies tend to vary and it is worth an in-depth study before commitment finally. The idea of parting with some of your hard-earned profit may well be repugnant to you but there are tremendous benefits which cannot be dismissed. Let us look at some of them.

In the context of this book, which is primarily written to help and advise those contemplating their first venture, the franchiser will give complete and total assistance in site selection, shop-fitting and equipping, staff training and advertising. They will supply you with a quality-controlled product with an already famous trade name and you will be part of an internationally-known network. You will, however, still be working for yourself which is the main attraction of being in business. During those first crucial weeks of 'shake-down' the franchiser will have his catering experts by your side coaching you and your staff until you can 'walk on your own'. My own feeling is that entering the catering industry at a time of madly escalating costs requires considerable business acumen to keep abreast of things. Therefore, for the newcomer to have behind him the expertise of a major company is an almost priceless asset.

The vital importance of good site selection and accurately assessing consumer need has been already recognised. Here the franchiser will be prepared to give assistance in finding and evaluating potential sites. They will not, however, license new outlets if, in their opinion, this would materially effect the business being done by one already existing locally. This is sensible because they are not only protecting themselves but you too. They will even, through their estates department, go to considerable lengths in negotiating difficult lease problems and, in certain cases, the purchase of a freehold. Once the site has been selected there comes the question of shopfitting. The company's technical department produces plans for the conversion and offers technical advice. There is not, at the time of writing, any charge for this service. The costs of shopfitting, and of the conversion, are borne by the licensee (or franchisee) and these, of course, can vary considerably. Such capital costs depend on several factors, such as the size of the operation – perhaps anything from 50 to 150 seats for example – and the type, locality and the country where it is to be set up. As a rough guide a sum of £20,000–£60,000 could be envisaged. Assistance is sometimes given in the form of free-loan equipment. In other cases it may be provided on hire purchase.

Some degree of uniformity must be expected with other establishments similarly franchised. In any case there are considerable marketing advantages since the franchisee's outlet will be consistent in form and appearance with the well-known brand name. The public know and recognise at once a standard with which they are familiar in other parts of the country.

Once fitted out the company's experts will assist in training the franchisee and his staff and stay until things are running well. Training is also given in book and record keeping, operation of V.A.T., etc. There is considerable promotional and advertising support initially, and again, provided free. All the experience and marketing expertise which probably the 'loner' will never acquire in a lifetime is there for the asking. Restaurateurs and caterers generally are, for the most part, individualists and like doing their own thing; I am one of those people. On the other hand, I have been a caterer for some fifty years and have a wide background of experience. If I were not, then I think I would very seriously consider taking on a franchise. The road of experience is a very hard one and nobody can deny the vast pool of knowledge that the big company has. To have all this behind you with its multifarious benefits in so many directions in exchange for a comparatively modest initial licence fee and franchise royalties cannot be bad but, as mentioned on page 21, do 'shop around' initially.

Naturally the franchiser is not in it for fun. He is selling more of his product by virtue of being your supplier and enlarging the scale of his operations. He will expect you to run your business efficiently and preserve the image of the brand name; it is a partnership in some ways, but only in a remote sense.

The 'Take-away'

If V.A.T. troubles you then a take-away form of business may attract you. Some of the larger franchisers also offer 'Take-away' operations. All the foregoing benefits of franchising apply in the same measure – site selection, fitting out, training, marketing and so on. It is an outlet for hot, high-quality foods. It satisfies an essentially local market in much the same way that fish and chip shops do, but offers such things as curry, barbecued spare ribs and chicken, pies and pasties and simple vegetables such as peas, pease pudding, coleslaw and beans. It is a form of merchandising which is growing very rapidly and continues to grow annually. Going back to our office workers for example, it is absolutely tailor-made for their requirements. If a 'Take-away' is set up on a site where there are attractions such as a dog race-track or dance hall, cinema, etc., it could prove a winner. The initial capital cost is usually much lower than the case of other franchises as no seating facilities, other than for the waiting customer, or tabling are required. The site area too does not need to be as large, small shop premises being quite sufficient. It is considered that a normal capital outlay and investment could be recovered in less than two years if owner operated or say, three years under management at present levels of profitability. This then is quite an attractive proposition and has very good marketing possibilities on the right site.

Trading hours can easily be tailored to meet local requirement but, to be successful, almost certainly evening trading
would be essential.

Fast Food Operations

Mention has been made on page 21 of 'franchised fast food
operations'. While a large section of this particular market is
franchised, it does not mean that a capable and imaginative
caterer cannot go his own way. There is great scope here for
original thinking in terms of 'product' and design of premises
as well as service. The changing social pattern of the last
decade has influenced the rapid growth of the 'fast food' outlet. It is almost an industry within the industry and the last few
years have seen the publication of its own trade journal and
even a trade exhibition. It tends to be specialised and I can
perhaps do no better than recommend that you read Peter
Bertram's *Fast Food Operations* (see page 185). Visit and
study existing operations – even a trip to America. Success
here, however, does mean choosing the right site with plenty
of passing trade. In the right hands it is one of the most
profitable facets of our industry.

Finally, whatever kind of catering establishment you decide
to operate it is very important to remember one salient point.
The catering industry is, in the main, a leisure industry. Not
leisure for the successful operator I fear, but catering for a
public that are at leisure. It is hard, tough and demanding but
unless you are prepared to meet the challenge of providing
food, beverages and liquor when the public need them, then
whatever form your business takes, it will never prosper. We
are a service industry in its fullest sense and we can only
progress if we satisfy the demand that is there. The public
through its growing affluence is eating out more than ever
before. It is more informed and selective than it has ever been.
Treat them right and maintain an honest policy, whether
trading high class, fast call-order, or cheap and popular, and
you will succeed.

CHAPTER 3

Kitchen Layout

Planning Considerations

The subject of kitchen layout is a very important one; indeed the kitchen is the nerve centre (rather an apt description!) of the operation. It is the hub of the business and, if not properly planned and carefully thought out, or with the wrong equipment installed for the job, can result in chaos at worst, or slow, costly, inefficient service at best. There are, of course, a very considerable number of factors to be considered. Two main requirements at once emerge and are distinctly separate. The first is the type and size of the equipment as dictated by the particular needs of the business to be done. The second is the workability and the arrangement of the equipment to facilitate maximum and optimum performance, permitting ease of operation and service. A third consideration of undisputed importance is the working environment of the staff employed there.

Let us consider essential number one. Reduced to its simplest form, and dependent on the style of business done, it would be quite feasible to install only three main items of equipment. A deep-freeze, a microwave oven and a service hotplate. This particular simple form of kitchen would be based on a specialised menu consisting solely of a bought-in range of ready-cooked frozen dishes and convenience foods. The kitchen, being designed round the menu requirement, would obviously be totally limited to performing only these tasks.

The main items of cooking equipment in a Wimpy Bar would be a griddle, toasters and fryer. Again the cooking facilities would be restricted to a call-order unit in full view of the customers and designed only to cope with simple menu demands. These then are two prime examples of simple requirements being entirely dictated by a conscious marketing policy. Once, however, the style of operation is changed to the traditional kind, then more equipment has to be installed in order to cope with the increased work-load and demand.

Kitchen Size

How big is the kitchen to be? To be a bit sweeping perhaps – nearly as big as the restaurant itself (architects please note). There are many cases where modernisation and modification of centres of public entertainment have been carried out and the kitchen space has been hopelessly inadequate. Cases where upwards of 250 diners were expected to be catered for with a five-course menu in a kitchen measuring fifteen foot square. In one example the washing-up facilities designed-in were one stone sink, and this where 120 people regularly sat down to a banquet-style meal – an almost impossible situation for the poor caterer and his staff. No wonder chefs are sometimes considered temperamental! There were actually complaints from the operators of the latter premises that some washing-up was being left until the next morning, thus encouraging vermin. If it were not so serious, it could almost be funny and yet, whilst these are perhaps extreme cases, they do happen. Hindsight is never good enough and, once building has been completed, very costly in terms of further alteration, even if room is available, which is not usually so. The work-load requirement of the kitchen, not forgetting possible future growth of trade, should always be studied very carefully. To put in more seats in the restaurant than the kitchen output can cope with is an invitation to disaster.

Utility Supply

Not only does the equipment have to be considered. The

supply also is something which is going to require careful study, such as the size of the gas feed and the capacity of the electrical switchboard. Some modern pieces of equipment, having emphasis on speed of production, can be very heavy in terms of power demand. A small high-output fryer for example sometimes requires as much as nine kilowatts. Put two of these side by side and you may well find that your existing supply is totally inadequate and that a new supply, more than likely three-phase, will have to be put in. Far better to do it when you start than later. My own advice based on much practical and hardwon experience in this particular field is always to put in a heavier gas and electricity supply than you think you will need. There is no harm in being an optimist and it is a lot cheaper in the long term, believe me. Not long after I started I blew the company fuse twice and each time on a Saturday afternoon in the winter. Our own fuses, such as they were, were almost welded into the holders! The result was of course complete rewiring throughout. When opening up a further extension some years later, the electricity board were puzzled why I wanted such heavy switching gear. I did not need it then, but I do now; I had learned my lesson.

Quality of Equipment

Never buy cheap equipment if you can possibly avoid it, even if it means a further visit to the bank manager. To expect a piece of equipment designed for domestic usage to stand up to the hurly-burly of the commercial kitchen is not really on. Once you start to employ staff in any number they will very quickly make this shortcoming evident. If you trade in a comparatively small way, and you yourself are the main user of the equipment then, knowing how much it cost you, you will look after it, keep it clean and well maintained; but the staff will not to anything like the same degree usually.

Commercial equipment is built to stand heavy and often continuous usage. Nowadays it is usually constructed of stainless steel and is clean and simple in design. It is always well worth shopping around before coming to a decision and never accept, as fact, paper claims. Examine it carefully and assess the performance in relation to its projected requirement what-

ever it is likely to be. I like to see the make and model being
used by the big companies in their own operations. If ordinarily it is good enough for them then it is going to be good
enough for me. Undoubtedly the best opportunity to see all
the equipment laid out side by side is a visit to Hotelympia.
This exhibition, which takes place every two years in January,
is as the name suggests held at London's Olympia. It is the
shop-window of the catering equipment industry and lasts for
ten days. There you will see every possible piece, shape and
size of equipment used and will be able to select what is right
for you. Do not be afraid to ask questions in plenty, however;
you are the buyer. Take measurements and soundly assess
suitability. Then go home and think about it before placing
a firm order.

Communications

The need for the main kitchen to be on the same level as the
dining area has been mentioned. This, based on practice, is
normally an accepted fact. There is a school of thought which
decrees that the kitchen should be on the top floor so that
cooking smells and fumes do not enter the restaurant. I only
subscribe to that view if the dining area is on the top floor too.
It is a comparatively simple matter to dispose of unwelcome
odours by proper ventilation and extraction, whereas the
difficulties of service from a kitchen to restaurant by lift are
legion.

The only exception, from a service standpoint, is possibly
where purely banqueting service is carried on. Then the passing of courses in bulk, as they are required, to a separate
service area is not uncommon. The placing of large numbers of
different orders by microphone or other means, and their
subsequent service by lift is slow, tedious and also requires
constant attendance to ensure quick removal of dishes to the
upper (or lower) service hotplate if there is one. In short, it is
complicated and difficult with rather remote communications.
The aim, when designing, should therefore always be to stream
service as much as possible to permit easy communcation and
economy of movement.

Service Area

Let us start with the service. Ideally the dining-room staff should have access to the kitchen service through 'in' and 'out' doors. These should be fitted with look-through glass panels at head height, kicking plates and made to open only in the required direction. They should also be asbestos lined and fire proofed. If the fire brigade should interest themselves in the premises this will be almost a certain requirement.

As far as the kitchen is concerned the dining-room staff are involved in three ways. They will want to place orders, they will want to collect them and they will require to deposit dirty crockery and glass as well as silver dishes. Both the service hotplate, where the food order is placed and subsequently collected, and the dishwash area should be immediately adjacent to the dining-room access and egress. As the 'dirties' will be brought from the dining room through the 'in' door it is logical to arrange the dishwash area on that particular side of the service. If this is not so arranged it will mean traffic of 'dirties' across the flow of orders from the hotplate with consequent waste of time and movement, as well as risk of collision and breakages. The sound of china and glass crashing is not good for business or the proprietor's blood pressure! The hotplates, or hot cupboards, should be placed in such a way as to permit sufficient easy movement of staff, by the waiters/waitresses on the one side and the kitchen staff on the other. Depending on the style of service it might be advantageous for the hot cupboards to have doors opening on both sides. This would permit the picking up of soup plates or bowls without bothering the chef for example or plates if full silver service is in operation. Some hot cupboards are equipped with plate dispensers on a spring-loaded principle which stores them in such a way that they are always easy to pick up from the top of a stack. These are more likely to be found in self-service cafeterias however.

Unless the soups are to be served in tureens in the case of a high-class restaurant they will almost certainly be stored and kept hot in what is known as a bain-marie. These are simply pots (usually one-gallon capacity) which are let into the top of the hotplate and either dry heated by electrical elements under them or by being immersed in hot water.

If our bain-marie is placed in a suitable position at one end
of the hotplate with the soup plates or bowls underneath, the
dining-room staff can help themselves without delaying the
chef. Portion control is easily effected by use of a standard-
sized ladle. This method of service speeds things up considerably and, remember, the longer the customer sits there waiting,
the lower the turnover of seating and earning capacity. The
way the hotplate service, and the servery itself, is laid out is
critical to overall smooth, efficient operation. How extensive
you make the servery is obviously dictated by the space available and the needs of the business. It might, for example, be
possible to incorporate 'still-room' facilities for the making and
service of beverages. The important thing, however, is to keep
it functional and uncluttered in order to maintain smooth,
fast and free-flowing service to the dining room. If it is not
possible to arrange the still room equipment, café set, etc.,
integrally, then ideally it should be as near to the 'out' door as
possible, perhaps in an adjacent room with a service counter.
Coffee is, however, often made in the restaurant itself by Cona
or similar method. Cold dishes, starters, salads and sweets will
be served from another point away from the hot section. In
these technological days, refrigerated counters are, of course,
frequently seen in use and can be planned into the service area.
Properly thought out then, the service area will take care of
the three main aspects of service, i.e. the placing of the order,
the storage of it until required to be served and the easy
disposal of dirty dishes, etc. after clearance from the table.
The flow through the service area is therefore clockwise.

Equipment Requirement

Because of the obvious diversity of the trade, it is difficult to
do anything but generalise and be purely hypothetical. The
equipment needs of one business, as we saw at the beginning
of this chapter, are quite different from another's. Cooking
ranges vary a lot in size and output, and indeed, in style. Gone
are the old coal-fired, solid top ranges of pre-war days: the
modern stainless steel-clad (or vitreous-enamelled) range is a
different, much less temperamental and dirty animal. There

are, of course, all kinds of automated devices which one is accustomed to finding on the modern, domestic range which are not so frequently found on the commercial counterpart: self-igniting gas rings, self-cleaning ovens, automatic timing devices and internal illumination, etc. Unless your business is small and you alone use the equipment do not bother with these. Commercial ranges are built to be staff-proof; they cannot be otherwise and have to be one hundred per cent functional. They can also be easy to clean and nice to look at by all means, but if they are to be long lasting and reliable they must be simple and rugged.

Disregarding the question for the moment of whether circumstances, or personal choice, dictate a choice of gas or electricity, or even oil or Calor gas, there are different types of cooking ranges to choose from. There is our old friend the solid top range which as its name suggests has a top of solid heavy iron and heating all over the cooking area, with solid concentric rings which can be lifted out to expose a single, very large, gas burner. Chefs of the old brigade particularly tend to like them, but I would not recommend their installation and use in a 'popular' restaurant where the menu is simple and lightweight in style.

In the case of the menu being short and simple the open-top range with its separate burners (or rings if electric) is a much more practical proposition. For hard work and sheer reliability the simpler the better, and experienced caterers will often go for what might appear to be old-fashioned in design. The instant heat and controllability of 'high-speed gas' is well known as a sales promotion point but certainly if, during a slack period, the odd order comes up, there is much to be said for it. It is useful for the range to be fitted with pot-racks overhead so that pots and pans are to hand.

Ovens

So far only the tops of the cookers have been looked at. Ovens, whether installed as part of a solid top, or an open range, are really much of a muchness. Some have two side burners, some have a single burner at the back and some underneath. It is simply a question of design and, although I have examples of both kinds with little or nothing to choose from in the way of baking performance, I tend to favour the back burner in giving a more even spread of heat. But so long as the oven gives a nice even spread it does not really matter.

There are, of course, modern developments which are worth mentioning. One particular type of considerable merit is the forced air convector oven. My own particular style of business does not necessitate much baking and roasting or I would have one without any doubt. There is not, of course, a boiling top, and the oven is usually mounted on legs at waist level. An electrically driven fan forces the hot air round inside the oven. It is possible to cook batches of totally differing kinds of food together without, strangely, any transference of taste – such as say, cakes and chickens, or cheese straws and roast beef. The cooking temperature is lower and food takes less time to cook. The only possible disadvantages are noise from the fan which tends to roar (this may now be improved) and the fact that it is purely an oven and therefore, as a piece of equipment, not so versatile as the more conventional range. Of course, the same can be said of the purely baking oven. It is, however, designed for a specific job of work with several compartments operating at different temperatures. A baking oven might be totally unnecessary in one business, but if another had a large afternoon tea trade well known for cakes and pastries, it could well be quite essential.

Oven Door Design

Should oven doors drop down or open sideways? I do not think that there is any doubt that the door which drops down level with the bottom of the oven is the most practical, particularly for female staff. It forms a very useful and necessary platform on which to pull out, or place on, heavy roasting cases or baking tins containing joints or braises. It then gives the cook a good opportunity to hold it really firmly if being removed to a table, or while just being checked for cooking progress. Remember the question of space however. If the door extends two feet when down, then the cook will want at least another three feet in which to bend down in. It means simply that if space is tight it would be contributory to an accident. In such a situation a pair of side-opening doors might require one foot less and be a sounder proposition.

Many professional cooks despise aids such as Regulo settings and one rarely finds these on the commercial oven. The senses of sight, touch and smell are usually the professional's Regulo, plus that irreplaceable item – experience. They used to say 'Put your hand in the oven to see if it is hot enough – if it turns black then it is too hot!'. If it singed the hairs it was about right! Do not think, however, that I am not progressive. Anything which makes the job easier and more efficient and is better for the staff to use, therefore increasing profitability and perhaps job satisfaction, I am all for it. It is simply that the rough and tumble of a busy commercial kitchen is vastly different from the home. Non-stick pans are a prime example unless, as we have already recognised, you yourself are going to see that they are properly used. Even then, will they stand perhaps twelve hours a day of continuous usage? I think not.

Grills

If you are going to make grills the main feature of your menu, then similarly there are many kinds to choose from. In the early days of my present business I went overboard for what was then the latest thing. The so-called electrically operated 'Infra-red Grill'. They are something of a misnomer and are really only 'contact' grills where the meats are cooked at high speed between two super-heated, ribbed, heavy metal plates giving contact on both sides simultaneously. This type of grilling equipment is still used in many small restaurants some twenty years after it was introduced into this country; it performs its task very quickly, cutting cooking time considerably, and leaves distinctive markings on the food simulating those of the traditional grill bars. They have the advantage, not only of speed, but of small space requirement. The disadvantages however, certainly in my own case, were that they were unreliable in heavy, continuous use over a twelve-hour operation and that in order to keep two serviceable I had to have four or five, since two were always being repaired. They also tend to carbonise on the cooking surfaces which involves a dirty job cleaning them with a wire brush. The use of 'Teflon' and similar non-stick coatings has eliminated this trouble. When the equipment is dirty it tends to create smoke and an acrid smell and needs to be well extracted. I have long since ceased to use these particular grills; in very heavy trading conditions they were more of a nuisance than an asset. However, I would consider the infra-red grill to be a reasonable proposition in a less demanding situation. If it is to be your sole means of grilling though, keep a spare!

The two other main types of grilling equipment are the underfired traditional model and the overfired grill which, in a slightly different form, is called a 'salamander'. To deal with the underfired type first: this, as the name suggests, cooks the food on open bars with the fire underneath. The days of the old coke-fired grill are almost over, for those may only be found occasionally in the famous, traditional grill rooms, and you would hardly be likely to want to acquire one. They call for a considerable amount of attention and expertise in operation and, in any case, scarcely fit into the modern scene. The old pre-war grill cook was somewhat different from his modern, crash-programme-trained and paper-hatted counterpart found in chain operated steak houses! However, be that as it may. The modern, underfired grill falls into two main categories: one has firebricks which are gas heated to a graduated degree, the hottest being at the back; the other is the simulated charcoal grill. In the case of the latter, specially prepared stones are heated by gas flames, not unlike the night watchman's brazier. In both cases the meats are cooked on open bars over the heat.

New examples of the first type are becoming increasingly difficult to find however. They are perhaps old fashioned in concept, and costly in terms of capital outlay and in running costs. It makes an excellent focal point for diners, and to see the grill cook at work. It is imposing and helps to create an authentic atmosphere. Cooking does require a greater degree of expertise than with other kinds of grill. If, however, you still favour the underfired grill then the simulated charcoal model is usually much cheaper and probably takes up a little less space although floor area is much the same. Claims for this type sometimes extend to a distinctive 'charcoal' flavour being given to the meat. The bars are sloped at a shallow angle in both cases to permit different degrees of cooking and disposal of fat.

Without doubt the most popular form of grilling equipment, either heated by gas or electricity, is the overfired grill or salamander. We had better first dispose of the distinction. It becomes a grill when it is fitted with a solid (usually ribbed), sloped metal plate and is therefore used for grilling meats. It becomes a salamander when fitted with a level, open-barred shelf on which fish is grilled, sauces glazed or toasted specialities finished, like Welsh Rarebit for example. It can also be used for making large quantities of toast, etc. It is quite possible to grill meats, of course, in this way as one does on a domestic cooker. It is usual, however, in commercial practice to use the solid plate supplied for the purpose. This quickly heats up, since it is usually of alloy, and to a large extent cooks the food on both sides, the heating source over the top (hence overfired) and the hot grill plate underneath.

Wherever the grilling equipment is sited considerable attention must be paid to ventilation and extraction. Apart from the fryers, there is no greater source of cooking smells and smoke. If they are not placed under the main kitchen canopy then they should have their own hood and extraction system. From a work routine standpoint the grill should be placed conveniently close to the main service hotplate and have a table or hotplate very close to it on which to 'dress up' finished dishes. Facilities are also necessary for storage of silver flats or plates. Everything should be readily to hand to avoid surplus movement, wasted time and energy. If 'plate service' is the vogue and the food not garnished on separate silver dishes it is logical to place the grill near the fryer since, almost inevitably, 'French Fries' will be served with the meats and other garnishes. Remember that longer grill tongs will be needed for the underfired grill of the 'Benham' type in order to reach meats placed at the back.

Fryers

The two main kinds of deep fryer are the larger and more traditional gas or electrically heated 'pans' and the fast-recovery, smaller, high-output electric-immersion heated

'Valentine', 'Turmix', or similar. The latter have found a very strong following in recent years with the growth of fast food outlets. They have certain limitations, one being the very heavy fuel consumption and wattage loading. If you consider installing this type of fryer please see that your switchgear and wiring is capable of accepting the load. Depending on the volume of trade you could well need two. If you intend to do a large amount of fish frying you will find that although the speed of cooking is fast, the actual capacity in terms of accept-ance of large pieces, such as fillets of plaice, is restrictive. They are really best dealing with a fast output of chips or small-sized items such as chicken, or scampi, etc. The two notable advan-tages are slim shape and small demand on valuable kitchen space and, as already noted, fast output and recovery of cooking temperature. However, only oil can be used for frying.

The more traditional fryer comes in many sizes of pan and is more versatile in ability to cope with a mixed trade. All modern fryers are thermostatically controlled and well de-signed and there are a large number of makes and models to choose from. When deciding finally, it is however important to anticipate the demands that the frying equipment will have placed on it. This is dictated primarily by the style of menu and also by whether, as a policy, you intend to use fresh or frozen chips. The frozen product will mean that you will not need to blanch chips before service starts. This reduces the load on the fryer considerably. It is also possible to use a solid vegetable frying fat as well as oil in this type, which is some-times an advantage economically. If the menu style suggests a fair proportion of fish frying then a pan, large enough to cope with say six or so fillets or pieces of fish at a time, as well as chips, will be necessary. If your equipment is too small it results in frustration in the kitchen and slow service. The equipment itself too becomes over-loaded and short lived. As with the grill good extraction is vital.

Boilers, etc.

So far the main items of fixed heavy equipment in the average restaurant kitchen have been dealt with. Service hotplates and bain-maries, ranges and ovens, grills and fryers. It is, however, conceivable that you may require to install boilers or steaming equipment. Once again the style of the menu will dictate the need. Usually these items are more likely to be found in larger kitchens dealing with mass feeding such as canteens or institutions. The average restaurant often finds it sufficient to use portable steamers in conjunction with the top of the stove. There are, however, quite excellent small, fixed steamers, usually gas operated, on the market. It might be useful to have a 25–30 gallon boiler or two for cooking large joints such as whole gammons, large-scale quantities of vegetables, or even for use as a stockpot. If, however, it is not proposed to use a fixed boiler for stockpot purposes it is useful to install a low, gas-operated, stockpot stand which is specially designed for this purpose or for making consommé. Lifting 15 gallons of stock, bones etc. up on to a normal range is heavy going, and I would not ordinarily recommend a fixed boiler for stock-making purposes. The stock tends to 'go off' overnight and they are more difficult to clean than one which you can take to the sink in the pot-wash.

Before dealing with movable equipment, it would be pertinent to consider layout a stage further now. The service area and flow of movement have been considered. Referring back, you will have noted a circular and logical sequence of operation. Just as this is very necessary on the other side of the hotplate, so is careful study and planning on the kitchen side. I find it rather pointless to draw diagrams because the area and shape of the available space that you will have are hardly likely to be the same; nor are you likely to have the same equipment needs. It is only possible to be hypothetical, taking due regard of customary practice. Most major kitchen equipment suppliers offer a planning and advisory service, which is often free. They will assist you to plan your kitchen in the most practical way consistent with space and menu needs. However, perhaps a few words of mine may help.

'Island' Layout and Canopy

Undoubtedly the most practical form of layout, from most standpoints, is what is termed as an 'island' kitchen. This means that all the major fixed heavy equipment will be grouped together in the centre, back to back, allowing for completely free movement of staff all round. Since most of the wall area will be free, except for movable pieces such as refrigerators, etc. and benches, the kitchen is easier to keep clean. Again, as such equipment is likely to be the most productive of cooking smells and heat, it can all be grouped under one overall canopy incorporating an efficient and powerful extraction system. The canopy, or skirt, should not be too low so as to prohibit the wearing of hats. Almost certainly it will have to be purpose-made either, preferably, of stainless steel, or of wired glass in a steel angle frame. It is a most important fixture and it is unwise to try to economise or do without it.

Routing Service

How the equipment is actually arranged will depend for the most part on the number of kitchen staff employed and how they are departmentalised, the style of service (i.e. whether silver or plate service), and the kind of menu. Obviously the stoves and grills should be near to the service hotplate and, preferably, either parallel or at right angles to it, so that dishes when completed can be passed straight to it for collection without having to walk right round the kitchen. Thought must be given to the sequence of operations so that staff are not working across each other and getting in each other's way, for this leads to frustration, wasting of time, confusion and is a source of accidents. Do not forget the sensible placing of tabling where it is needed. Any equipment such as the fryer must also be situated conveniently near to the hotplate.

In simple terms, therefore, all the equipment likely to be in constant steady use should be arranged in such a way as to be conducive to fast service by as short a route as possible having regard for the flow and sequence of cooking. Items such as steamers, boilers and anything else not of immediate requirement should be installed at the back of the 'island'. On the face of it this is merely common sense, but unless one properly visualises practical routing before everything is installed, or even when adding new equipment, the smooth flow in the kitchen can be seriously disrupted. Try to think in terms of a production line and lay out the equipment accordingly. If, as is usually the case, the French Fries (chips) are going to be put on to the plate last, then obviously it would be foolish to install the fryer at the opposite end of the service. If you, yourself, are not too sure then seek the opinion of your chef or cook. Go through the motions and think about them carefully. If, unfortunately, you are not able, for reasons of cramped space, to arrange your equipment in a centre island but round the wall, make sure that there is a sufficient gap round the back and sides to permit cleaning. Nothing attracts vermin like grease and stale pieces of trapped food. Whether round the walls or in the centre, however, the same principles of work flow apply in equal measure.

Tabling

The kitchen should contain sufficient tables and work benches, arranged either parallel to, or flanking the stoves. If the restaurant is large enough to employ a full brigade in the kitchen then each department should have its own tabling and workspace. Even if the operation only requires a single-handed chef or cook, he should have a table near to his stove work. Hygiene regulations require that work-tops should have impervious surfaces. Even laminates such as Formica get chipped and lift from the wood underneath, leaving spaces and crevices to harbour filth and dirt. The only answer in a commercial kitchen are tables and benches with stainless steel tops mounted on galvanised steel frames and legs with adjustable feet. They should be fitted with drawers, often made of alloy with metal racks underneath on which to place objects such as sieves or whatever is required for service. Try to avoid wooden benches if you possibly can and particularly avoid securing them to the wall. It should always be possible to move them out to clean behind.

Refrigeration

Refrigeration is something you can never ever have enough of. When starting, the soundest advice I can give is to buy a refrigerator twice as big as you think you will want. Quite a lot of foodstuffs need to be put away at night when service is finished. This keeps food fresh, of course, and avoids waste and vermin. The modern refrigerator is an excellent piece of mechanism requiring very little attention, not even periodic defrosting, this function being automatic. Often there is not even a need to empty water away after the defrosting process has taken place since it is evaporated. This is a great boon. The 'sealed unit' motor likewise requires little attention and is hardly worth putting on a maintenance agreement. I would not say the same however of the older type of equipment.

The placing or planning of your refrigeration is a question of where it is needed and the system of work. As a matter of principle, and to give the equipment a chance to work efficiently, it should be away from the heat of the kitchen. There are exceptions however, and one is where a large grill trade is done. To save time in passing the orders from the larders, if there is one, to the grill cook, it is useful for him to have a working stock close at hand. This is not kind to the equipment, but it is not kind to meat left out otherwise in the heat, either. The only practical working solution is to install a small refrigerator as convenient as possible to the grill. Where the grilling is carried out in a public situation and in view of the diners, the usual system is to have an open refrigerated display cabinet. This does the double duty of allowing the client to choose his own steak or chop, and keeps it in good condition too. If you do decide to adopt this idea, be sure you specify quite clearly the purpose for which you want the cabinet or you may finish up with a model with a higher temperature range which would be unsuitable.

Refrigerators come in all shapes and sizes so it is an easy matter for you to choose the one (or two, or more) best suited to you. There are models which are tall and slim in shape, but still offering a very workable, and useful, twenty cubic feet of capacity for example. This particular shape and capacity is just about ideal for a small café or restaurant.

Extensions of refrigeration are of course a cold room and, that modern, indispensable adjunct to catering, the deep-freeze cabinet and its close relative the ice cream conservator. If the size of the business warrants it, of course, a sizeable cold room is well worth its weight. If you have a small existing room, or space, any firm of refrigeration engineers will build in a tailored unit by insulating the floor, walls and ceiling. The unit can be housed remotely and, in this connection, it is a good idea to site it outside in the fresh air, if you have a yard, where it can work efficiently. The shelving can be made up to whatever widths and length or spacing you require. It is, therefore, a good idea to measure the sizes of box tins, or whatever trays or containers you are most likely to use, and then specify the shelving accordingly. You will then make the most efficient use of the available space.

Freezers

Deep-freezes are marketed in two main types, upright with normal front opening door and the deep chest. Both are efficient enough but the upright cabinet is much more useful if items are likely to be required quickly and fairly frequently, such as packets of vegetables, prawns, etc. If such small packages are stored in the deep, chest cabinet it often means difficulty and searching, and what is wanted is usually right at the bottom. If, on the other hand, you are going to store foods that will only be required infrequently, or have been laid down in times of plenty and cheap price, then there is no problem. The upright type is more economical of floor space, but it is not really suitable for the storage of large joints. Both types have their uses and you will know what suits your own particular needs best.

In the case of the average restaurant, probably the upright cabinet is best. It is customary for suppliers of frozen foods to offer such cabinets of either type on freeloan or cheap rental for three years when, ultimately, it becomes a free loan. It should not, therefore, be necessary to purchase, although a certain sales figure guarantee is sometimes required. This is not usually very high however. The same applies to ice cream conservators. A sales contract is drawn up which naturally restricts the buyer to the one source of supply and the company does not, as a rule, like to find other goods like frozen fish fillets in their ice cream cabinet. Such cabinets are usually on free loan however. It is always wise to check on the position of losses should the cabinet break down and the necessary insurance against such contingencies is cheap and easy to arrange.

Sweet Preparation Area

Depending on the size of the business and the premises it may be possible to have a pastry or sweet preparation department. If this is the case then, since all the sweets, melbas, etc., will be made up for service there, the ice cream conservator will be so placed. Similarly the cold room, and possibly the deep-freeze will be situated in the larder where the butchery, etc. is carried out. Both departments will ideally flank the main kitchen and be on outside walls where sufficient windows will help to keep the working environment cool.

Vegetable Preparation Area

If it is possible, a vegetable preparation room, which can be combined with salads, etc., should be included in the plan. The equipment here would consist of an electric potato-peeling machine, possibly an electric or hand-operated chipper, a machine for shredding and cutting and a deep sink or two. A quarry tiled floor with drainage gulley is also a practical necessity. Potato-peeling equipment comes in many sizes. There is a temptation to buy a model which is too small when starting. The larger the capacity, the less time the operation takes, a fourteen- to twenty-eight-pound capacity would ordinarily be quite large enough in the case of a 50- to 100-seat restaurant. The floor of the 'Veg Prep' should be fitted with wooden slatted stands on which to store potatoes at least six inches clear of the floor to avoid wetness. Wire racks or bins should be installed for green and root vegetables and shelving for storage of boxes, e.g. lettuce, tomatoes, etc. Finally, sufficient work-top space on which to cut and prepare. Drainage and water supply are important in this section which should be opening on to the main kitchen but, if possible, near or adjacent to the back yard for deliveries and removal of waste.

Plate-wash Area

The plate-wash operation must be designed with the same conception of 'flow' as any other department involved in service. The speedy and hygienic processing of dirty crockery, glass and cutlery plays a very important part in the general organisation. The plate-wash area, as we have seen, should be conveniently near to the 'In' service door from the restaurant so that the dirties can be disposed of quickly by the dining-room staff. A 'reception bench', preferably of stainless steel, should be immediately to hand on which to stack. Since a certain amount of plate waste, bones, etc., will be evident, it is always practical to have a ten-inch hole cut in the top of the bench so that a bin or bucket can be placed underneath to receive the swill. If the hole is lined with thick rubber, damage to the plates will be avoided if they are knocked. Rubber spatulas are useful for plate scaping. The proper scraping of the plates makes a considerable difference to the washing-up operation, particularly in keeping the water clean.

At right-angles to the reception bench there should be a feed-in table to the machine itself. On this will be placed the particular type of trays, or racks, that the machine uses. In the larger type of commercial model it is normal to use square, fitted trays which pass through and when the cycle is completed out of the other side. Smaller models often have segment fitted racks which, working on a rotary washing principle, need to be lifted in and out. In both cases the crockery, or other pieces, are washed by high pressure water jets going through a wash and subsequently a rinse cycle. In most modern machines this is entirely a timed, automatic procedure, the wash temperature being at about 140°F. and the rinse at about 180°F.

The final rinsing process having finished, the clean items will be passed from the machine directly on to another table to dry. If the machine is operating correctly with clean water at the right temperature, the crockery should be ready to stack away without further attention. Glass and cutlery will, however, more often than not require polishing. There should be sufficient storage shelving for the clean items to be put away immediately or be ready to be taken straight back into service.

Thus the 'flow' is reception and scraping, passing through the washing machine, drying and polishing, putting away or passing back into service – the whole operation being planned to ensure a minimum of movement by the operator.

No mention is made of sink washing-up as I do not think that in this enlightened age a restaurant, however small, should try to manage without machine washing. It is necessary on health grounds alone since the law, whilst not entirely specific, but certainly in spirit, requires protection of the public. Emphasis is placed nowadays on sterilisation and the avoidance of using cloths as much as possible. Labour cost too is cut if machine operation saves a second washer-up. In this connection the capital cost of the machine could well be saved in less than a year. A sink, or pair of sinks, is however a practical necessity in the platewash area for soaking stubborn items for example and for general purposes.

Machine Performance

In my experience whenever a machine fails to do its job properly it is because of one of two things. Lack of attention by the operator to simple daily maintenance tasks and through not changing water at the specified intervals, or the use of an unsuitable detergent. The question of what is the right detergent often depends on the degree of harshness in the local water supply. Consult your supplier. In hard water areas a water softener is often a good investment. Automatic dispensing of detergents is also cost saving. The equipment can often be fitted by the detergent suppliers. It is wise to keep the platewash machine on a maintenance agreement with the manufacturer to ensure reliability.

Pot-wash

The last kitchen department is the 'pot-wash'. Again this should be arranged conveniently so that disposing of dirty saucepans, or fetching clean ones, does not necessitate walking too far. The sinks should be of stainless steel and also of a deep commercial type since a domestic sink will not be deep enough for washing large pots or big box tins, etc. It goes without saying that there should always be an abundant supply of hot water. The pot-wash should be fitted with pot-racks of galvanised steel so that pans and tins can all be systematically stored away after washing. If the kitchen is being newly and purpose planned, it would be logical to place the pot-wash adjacent to the plate-wash to facilitate plumbing and drainage which can then be common to both. Again, automatic dispensing of detergent means economy.

We have dealt with the main departments and most of the heavier equipment that you will need. There is still much that you will need before you serve your first meal however. Again the qualification of the 'needs of the business' must be the overriding factor. If you are going to use all 'bought-in' sweets, for example, and never serve mashed potatoes, it may not be necessary to buy a food mixer.

Saucepans

Assuming a normal varied menu, the following items of small equipment will be needed. A range of heavy-duty saucepans from half pint upwards. Ensure that you have sufficient. You do not want to have to rewash a pan every time it is needed for an order or for any other purpose when you are under pressure. Do not try and economise on quality.

I will not waste much space on copper. It looks wonderful when properly maintained and the real professional likes nothing better but, not only does it cost a fortune in capital outlay, the costs of constant retinning and the labour of keeping it clean are not really on in the eighties of this century. Again, stainless steel saucepans have never really caught on in the trade; they are inclined to be expensive and to warp on occasions.

The commercial, heavy-duty, aluminium alloy saucepan has been found to be the best compromise. It has its drawbacks of course. The most common criticism of aluminium is its tendency to turn white sauces and soups grey in colour. Only be an infinitesimal quantity, tiny particles of the alloy rubbed off in over-exuberant whisking, causes this trouble. Cheaper alloy saucepans tend also not to stand up to knocks and, because it is a soft metal, handles work loose and come off. It therefore pays to buy the best and tell the cook to take the whisk out and use a wooden spatula as much as possible. I would not like to make Hollandaise Sauce with a spatula however! You can always keep another vessel such as a tinned bowl, especially for that sort of thing.

Frying Pans

The only kind of frying pan really worth considering, and particularly omelette pans if we include them in this category, are those made of black iron. They will not only last a lifetime but always give good results with an even spread of temperature, thus turning out a well-cooked dish. Such items are not always easy to find and a specialist in hotel kitchen equipment, such as Leon Jaeggi Limited, will be the best source of supply.

The recognised way of cleaning a black iron omelette pan incidentally is to put some salt, preferably granulated, in the pan, expose it direct to the heat and let it burn. Give it a good rub out then with a piece of sacking, grease it and it will be non-stick. You can do this with a heavy black iron pan, but do not try it too often with one of domestic quality and weight.

Microwave Oven

You may well consider the need for a microwave oven. In a fast, busy trading situation, and particularly where the use of pre-cooked food is the vogue, it becomes indispensable. In my view it is essentially an adjunct and not the complete answer, unless your trade and menu is geared one hundred per cent to it. It cannot roast, grill or fry; it is, therefore, limited to a form of poaching and very fast reheating. You can, of course, perform all manner of tricks with it which are not in the best culinary guides. That, however, is a matter of conscience and experience.

A microwave oven is an expensive piece of equipment. Any tray or dish containing an element of metal cannot be used or it will cause shorting out and possible damage. Glass, plastics or earthenware are the answer. It can go wrong and be very costly to service and repair. Personally I prefer to hire but that is a matter of opinion. It is, however, a very useful thing to have and assists considerably in speeding up service times and, sensibly planned in conjunction with the menu, it is labour-cost saving.

Other Equipment

If you intend to make your own soups then a soup-machine, or triturator, is useful. This is a labour-saving item and avoids the need to push purée type soups through a strainer which is often wasteful of ingredients and quite a hard, long job.

Apart from items such as mincers which are often an attachment to the food mixer and perhaps a meat or bacon slicer, there only remains the small equipment. Here again, if you want good cooking results and long life from it, it pays to buy the best. An aluminum roasting or baking tin, for example, will warp badly and food will stick. It will dent easily and generally will not stand up to heavy use. A black iron roasting case will give a lifetime's use and better cooking results. True it is much heavier to handle but, because of its weight, gives a much more even cooking process. The roasting case too is deeper and is ideal for braising meats, oxtail, etc.

Baking sheets too are best when made of plain sheet steel and kept well greased. Pie dishes, flan tins and rings and shallow-sided trays will take care of meat or fruit pies and tarts. Some care should be taken to study sizes here to effect portion control. A twelve-inch pie dish would yield twelve portions of steak pie, a fifteen-inch sixteen portions for example. A sixteen inches by twelve inches by one inch deep tray would yield twenty-four portions of fruit tart. Once the normal level of trade is known it is easier to control production and avoid wastage.

Small Items

The sizes of ladles too effect portion control, particularly in the service of soup, the normal quantity being a standard half pint. Ladles are most practical in stainless steel. Perforated ladles are available for service of peas and beans, as are also large serving spoons. Triangular and square slices are for general use. Wire whisks can be had in various lengths, sizes and weights, a fairly heavy whisk being required for thick sauces. They should also be of a length consistent with the size of pots to be used. A whisk which is too small will be constantly slipping down and becoming immersed in the soup or sauce. Conversely, lighter whisks are needed for whipping cream or making mayonnaise, where there is no electric food mixer. Small six-inch lightweight whisks are wanted for omelette making and sundry stove work. A range of wooden spatulas and spoons should complement these.

Cooks ordinarily carry their own knives as the tools of their trade, but I should not rely on this. A full range of kitchen knives of good quality for chopping, peeling and carving is a prerequisite. Having the right tool for the right purpose is vital to the proper finish of the dish and, indeed, to economy. A joint, for example, carved with the wrong knife will yield many portions less than it should, thus reducing profitability considerably.

There are two kinds of strainers. The type most commonly used is the conical, perforated metal chinois, so called because of its resemblance to a Chinese hat. It is usually used in conjunction with a suitably sized ladle which, inserted inside, is used to push the liquid through by a pumping action. It is useful to have a strong wooden triangle to rest over the top of the saucepan. This firmly holds the chinois in position while the liquid is being passed. Such wooden triangles are also used to rest hot pans on when transferring from stove or oven to the kitchen table. Strainers of the second type are of wire mesh and not as robust, but they have the advantage of passing liquids quicker and easier. They will, however, permit the passage of small particles which can be detrimental to appearance.

A sufficient number of chopping boards should be available for preparation work. Nowadays, Environmental Health Officers show a distinct preference for the use of synthetic boards which do not support bacterial growth. However, if wood is used, select boards made in one piece, and the thicker the better, so that it withstands the occasional planing. Lighter weight boards can of course be used for items of preparation such as cutting tomatoes and salad stuffs, dicing vegetables, etc. Boards are required for pastry work but a marble slab is often preferred by the professional.

The paraphernalia of small equipment in a kitchen is endless but sieves are a necessary item. Again there are two types, the hair sieve for pastry work and the wire mesh for general work such as making breadcrumbs, passing pâté or purées, etc. These are available in various sizes according to requirement and a range of three is useful to have, say eighteen inch, twelve and fifteen inch to cover most needs.

Finally a tin opener: without question the best type is the rotary 'Bonzer' which is bench fitted. It will handle nearly all catering size cans, with only the most awkward, dead square types causing some difficulty, for year after year. Changing wheels and blades periodically is a simple matter and nothing has been marketed in recent years to approach its robustness and practicability.

As was stated at the beginning of this chapter, the kitchen is the hub of things. It is where the reputation of the business begins and ends, because the public are more conscious of what is on the plate than the chair they are sitting on. This being so, and I am sure this is right, then the efficiency of the kitchen is paramount. In this connection the efficiency of the chef or cooks is not in question. If he, or she, is a first-class craftsman then it will not be possible to turn out a good dish with unsuitable equipment in badly planned surroundings. Even a small kitchen can be planned in such a way that it permits the proper and sensible flow of service and if, above all, the limitations are considered carefully when the menu is thought out. You cannot do the impossible. If you try to, then the result will be chaotic and the turnover of staff very rapid. A careful balance of all the factors mentioned has to be preserved.

Food Hygiene Regulations, 1970

As part of the Food and Drugs Act, the Food Hygiene (General) regulations, 1970 affect both the planning and the operation of the kitchen and service. The regulations should, therefore, be carefully read and understood by all engaged in the supply and handling of food to the public. The spirit of the regulations is to avoid risk to health and, in this connection, there are basically two aspects. The first is that the structural condition of the kitchen should be hygienic. That is to say that walls, floor and ceilings should not only be kept in a good state without say, cracks or peeling surfaces, but be easy to keep clean. Whilst a good, clean, painted surface would be acceptable, ceramic tiles are the usual answer although these must be kept in good condition. Quarry tiles make the best floor surface and should incorporate open drain gulleys which are kept covered with metal grilles and are easy to clean out. Canopies over cookers must also be kept clean and are usually either of stainless steel or Georgian wired glass in metal framing. Work surface should be impervious. In this connection laminates are not the answer, particularly where they can lift from the wood underneath and trap filth. Again, stainless steel benches are the only real answer. Chopping blocks and cutting boards have to be kept planed and smooth and free from cracks. Ample sinks must exist for the satisfactory washing of utensils and equipment, and in this connection an ample and constant supply of running hot water should be available.

Whilst there is no legal objection to the washing of crockery, glass and cutlery by hand, only a machine can really do so effectively, washing at 140°F and rinsing finally at 180°F.

Food Storage

Food stored, or held for service, is also subject to regulations to the extent that, very broadly speaking, temperatures of not less than 145°F (62·7°C) in a hot cupboard or not more than 50°F (10°C) in the case of foods which must be kept cool are to be observed. There are exceptions, but these include items such as bread, butter, margarine, etc. The temperatures apply particularly to dishes containing meat, fish, gravy and cream. A 'made-up' meat dish can very quickly 'go off' and cause food poisoning for example if left out in a lukewarm state. Foods must also be kept covered, except those of course which are subject to immediate service.

Food Handlers

There must be a wash hand basin or sink installed with a supply of hot and cold running water, towels, nail brushes and soap. The subject of first-aid equipment is covered elsewhere but cuts must be properly treated and, of course, no food handler suffering from anything contagious should be allowed to work on food preparation and handling.

It is not possible in the space available to deal exhaustively with the Food Hygiene Regulations. The point has, I hope, been made that they are very pertinent to the proper operation of a catering establishment. Visits are made by Public Health Inspectors from time to time. In my experience they are not unreasonable people and will always give the establishment a chance to carry out their recommendations. They do have power to recommend closure to the magistrates however. As has been remarked elsewhere in this book, such publicity is not desirable.

CHAPTER 4

Restaurant Layout and Equipment

Planning Capacity

The question of what constitutes the best layout for a restaurant is a mixture of practicability, character and ambience. Few traditional restaurant dining rooms are the same and most bear the stamp of individuality. Once again, and inevitably, the style of business done is a very decisive factor in the choice of furnishings, fixtures and fittings, lighting and so on. Basically, however, the needs are always the same – a table to eat at and a chair to sit on.

Planning the seating capacity can be a very interesting exercise. Whilst it should not be the aim to cram all the available space so that it is uncomfortable both for customers and staff alike, remember that your seating capacity is your 'pay load'. If you should find yourself in the happy and enviable position of turning trade away, then four extra seats being turned over four times per day at a 'spending power' of £5.00 per head would mean £480.00 per six day being lost. Over £24,960 turnover per annum! In practice it probably would not happen, but it serves to illustrate the point. Referring back to Chapter 3, however, remember also that the kitchen will have to cope.

Table Arrangement

Disregarding the quality of the seating and tabling for the

moment, we will consider the question of spacing. The ideal width is twenty-four inches for each cover. A cover is the trade term for a 'lay up' for one person. This gives sufficient elbow room without cramping although it is possible to manage with twenty-one inches in a situation where customer comfort is not such an important consideration.

Fixed, back-to-back banquette or bench seating is, as a rule, less space consuming than separate chairs. One of the problems with this type of seating is the question of sharing on a four-seater table. It invariably means that the first diners will sit on the inside and will then, if joined by others, have to ask to be let out. Bench seating does, otherwise, help to create some kind of privacy and it can be helpful to place a jardinière or a wrought-iron grille between the backs, thus providing both atmosphere and interest. It also lends itself to be fitted right along one wall. The illusion of privacy can then be further extended by the formation of bays of seating, without losing more than perhaps the three-inch thickness of a screen. The seating, being fixed of course, does not allow for any flexibility and this can be a disadvantage should you wish to do any party catering requiring a more formal lay up.

My personal preference is for a mixed plan of banquettes and loose tables and chairs. Once again our old friend the compromise situation, but it does give the best of both worlds and gives clients a choice, as well as creating an interesting and less rigid appearance for the room. Most shopfitters will be more than willing to give assistance with your planning once they know the type of thing you are aiming for, and will usually draw up plans free.

Chairs

The type of chair chosen, as well as its quality, will obviously be a matter of personal choice and suitability for its particular purpose and class of trade. Whether upholstered in velour or other expensive fabric, plain wood or perhaps with pallet cushions, remember that the chair will have to stand up to a great deal of hard use. It must, therefore, be robust and well made, and see that it gives proper support. I have heard the old adage 'Don't make them too comfortable or they will stay too long!'. I don't believe it. The style of chair will have to tie in with the general ambience and match up with the overall quality of the other furnishings. In a good class establishment 'carving' chairs with arms give a quality appearance and a comfortable atmosphere. Even twenty-five per cent only of the total seating will help create this.

Lastly, of course, come stacking chairs. Whilst it is true that these can sometimes be poorly designed and with an appearance which at once substantiates their purpose, there are some very well-made and presentable chairs on the market which are also nicely upholstered in high quality materials. As extra chairs to bring out occasionally, particularly for functions, they are a very practical proposition, for storage is always a problem when space is tight. Like most dual-purpose things, however, there is always a tendency to shortcomings in one direction or another and it is worth shopping around to get the type which will fit in best and give most comfort.

Tables

Tables are obtainable in all kinds of specifications. Square, round, oblong and even those specially fitted so that they can be locked together to form a special shape, such as a horseshoe. Some have polished wood tops, some laminated plastic, green baize or leatherette with a thin foam underlay. The latter being known as a 'dead cloth' and only used in conjunction with a table cloth. It prevents the cloth slipping and is sound-deadening when the dishes are put down. Mats are used on polished wood table tops; but beware of plastic ones which stick to hot plates.

Whether to put in any particular shape of table or not is really a matter of the physical dimensions and shape of the room itself. Where banquette seating is installed, then square tables for two, or oblong seating four or six covers, are the only practical type as the seating is straight and fixed. It will, of course, adapt nicely to a corner situation. For the popular-price type of business, centre pedestals can be bolted to the concrete floor thus eliminating problems with table legs and also allowing easier access. Round tables are very useful since extra chairs can be placed around and, with our twenty-four inch cover, this means that six can be comfortably seated and spaced at a four-feet diameter table. Four (or five covers) can be accommodated round a three-feet diameter table. This gives you a certain amount of flexibility. The most important thing to remember, however, is that the diner, when seated, will occupy at least twenty-one to twenty-four inches of floor space from the table. In simple terms this means that a three-feet round table needs four feet all round for chair space and, additionally to be comfortable a further two feet all round for service. Something like an area seven feet square in theory. In practice, however, the service space surround will be shared with the next table thus halving the requirement.

If the tables are packed too tightly it means discomfort and lack of privacy for the customer and frustration and difficulty for the waiter or waitress. If hors d'oeuvre, sweet or liqueur trolleys are to be used in service then sufficient tolerance must be allowed for their easy passage round the room. This also applies, of course, to carving, or other wagons, used for flambé work. An oblong table for four can measure three feet six inches minimum, but should not be less than two feet in width. Two feet six inches is, for the sake of only six inches, surprisingly more comfortable and about ideal. It is entirely a question of inches quite often whether an extra table can be brought in or not. The height of the table is important and twenty-nine to thirty inches is about right for comfort.

Banquet tabling

If party catering or banquet work is envisaged a practical consideration is to install a locking table system. The master tables can then do ordinary restaurant duty, and when required leaves can be fitted in to make up longer sections as needed. The manufacturers of such systems offer quite complex arrangements with, for example, semi-circular ends to make up an oval, or segments for a horseshoe or open-centre round table. Legs are sometimes made to fold away, making for easy storage. Many finishes can be supplied. It is, in my view, a very practical and flexible system and thoroughly worth consideration as initial equipment should you consider it necessary.

Stations and Sideboards

One important factor which must not be overlooked is how the room is to be divided up into 'stations' for the service staff. Quite obviously the number of staff employed and the degree of expertise required of them is dictated by the style of business. One would not expect to find a head waiter, or chef de rang, serving egg and chips in his tail suit in a popular café! All the same, and even in a middle-class dining room, the same principles of organisation are necessary to some extent. In this connection the room needs to be divided up into sections in order to share the work load equally. The more elaborate the style of service, then the fewer the diners who can be efficiently dealt with by a waiter or waitress. This is only one of the reasons why prices are higher in a restaurant giving that kind of service. An establishment offering a straightforward menu with plated meals will probably only require one waitress for up to sixteen to twenty diners spread over four to six tables of mixed numbers, fours and twos. This is not hard and fast because of other factors but, to give reasonable service, this is as much as she will be able to cope with efficiently, in an average situation under normal pressures. In the case of full silver service with perhaps the necessity to prepare flamed dishes, or say, fillet Dover Soles etc., then a station waiter aided by one, or even two commis (assistants), would be essential.

Whatever the elaboration or otherwise, however, a sideboard or 'dummy waiter' is necessary for each station. These should be commercially designed with baize-lined, sectioned, pull-out drawers for cutlery and, underneath, sufficient room for side plates, glasses, cups and saucers, condiment materials such as oil and vinegar, sauces, pepper mills, etc. The top of the sideboard should be large enough to place trays on for clearance of dirties and heat-proofed so that hot dishes will not damage. Depending on the style of service, and the number of staff employed to be consistent with it, the restaurant can then be planned. A sixty seater would require at least four stations, possibly five, as a general guide but it is difficult to give much better indication due to the factors involved. The important thing is to ensure that the proper facilities are installed for the work to be done. A storage cupboard should be conveniently arranged for keeping reserve table cloths and serviettes, etc.

Décor

Decoration is perhaps something very personal, like choosing a picture or a hat. The manner in which the restaurant is arranged and decorated will at once create the atmosphere and set the scene. It could be a simple wallpapering job and a 'lick of paint', or a major design involving a small army of shop-fitters. You will have your own ideas as to what kind of atmosphere and ambience you wish to create and, above all, what you can afford to do. Whatever you do, please remember the practicalities. It is no good creating a Greek temple if the pillars are going to be a constant obstacle to service and perhaps take up half of the workable floor space. Personally I have my doubts about too much gimmickry. The public will come out of curiosity of course but unless the food matches the expectations of the décor, they will not return very often. As far as wall finishes are concerned, it is always wise to invest in something long term. A mixture of stonework and panelling, and even natural brickwork, if it is old and restored, all give character. If a wallpaper is chosen then buy the best, heavy duty and washable. A vinyl flock paper always looks warm and luxurious and whilst initially expensive, as long as it is protected where traffic is heavy, will last for up to twenty years. You may feel that this is a long time and a change is desirable more frequently than that, but it is well to remember that to redecorate too often could mean closing down for periods, with loss of business. A popular café might well get away with a wall finish such as laminated plastic board but these tend to look cold and can sweat badly with condensation if the ventilation is not too good. There are many wood-finish wallboards on the market nowadays and these are excellent but perhaps a little domestic in quality. They therefore need to be well battened to the wall, or fixed directly to it by adhesive if the original surface is smooth enough. The walls can even be given a rough finish with a special plaster technique, thus requiring only a coat of emulsion every year. In this case, false beams can be incorporated to give a period atmosphere –

completed with a few brasses. Whatever the wall covering though, it should be practical for its purpose, in character with the style of business, and long term. The initial impact of the décor on a customer is very important, so do not skimp.

Ceilings

As far as ceilings are concerned, these can contribute very considerably to the ambience. The ceiling can incorporate much of the lighting, perhaps concealed behind draped sections and curtains, or have 'pot lights' inserted in it. It can be very elaborate, or just flat, straight and plainly finished with emulsion. Again, try to visualise the problems of redecoration and particularly of the servicing of the lighting system. If the room has a very high ceiling you may wish to consider dropping it a few feet. This would allow for installation of extraction or air conditioning.

Air conditioning is something which, whilst expensive to install, is often not given anything like the consideration it merits. Restaurants do get unbearably hot on occasions, particularly when they are full and busy and can be very uncomfortable for customers and staff alike. It is something that in general we tend to neglect too much. It is, of course, possible to rent air conditioning plant which can be a fairly simple installation if the premises adapt easily. It is well worth looking into if you are to consider comfort as an important consideration.

Floor Surfaces

Carpets, a polished wood floor or thermoplastic tiles? I once even had a flagstone floor in a cellar dining room. This is perfectly in character as the walls are natural brick and flint-stone, and the furniture Tudor in style. The considerations are the same as with all the other furnishings, fixtures and fittings. Put in what is right for the job! When starting, of course, there is always the tendency (and the necessity) to look at every penny of capital. If capital is tight then the temptation is to economise. There is one area where this just is not viable, and that is carpets. Take my tip: if you cannot put down a heavy-duty, top quality Wilton or Axminster of 'contract' weight, then do not bother. Anything less will wear out in no time and be a threadbare disgrace to your establishment. Far better to wait till you can afford the right thing.

Whilst many carpets are of 27in. widths sewn together, I have always found that they tend to wear or give trouble at the seams unless of really first-class fitting and manufacture. A possible improvement on this method is the heat treatment which can be used for joining widths, but 'broadloom' is generally the best proposition. These can be obtained in very generous although varying widths, and whilst some sewing might well be necessary seem to give very little trouble in service. Go to a supplier who specialises in hotel or contract carpeting. Your carpet will have to stand up to very heavy use (and misuse) so choose something suitable. A plain carpet always tends to show stains and gets 'patchy' with faded areas possibly. A carpet with a strong pattern and a few dark colours in the design will prove the most practical in use. It is an expensive item and you will need to look after it, but the question of maintenance will be discussed under a later heading.

Whilst there is little doubt that a carpet does give a restaurant of the right type the necessary degree of comfort and appearance, there are many other floor coverings and surfaces which must rank for consideration. However, the kind of flooring which already exists will influence the choice. It is really a waste of time and money to consider putting down asbestos thermoplastic tiles unless the floor is concrete with a properly screeded finish specially prepared to receive them. Once down then they will be good for years of use. A quite attractive tile is now available in a natural cork finish. This has a clear, tough, vinyl surface which allows the cork to show through and not only looks well but wears well too. It does not like smouldering cigarette ends though, whereas the asbestos tile is not damaged.

Asbestos or thermoplastic tiles require attention in the way of sealing and polishing and unless properly treated can become slippery and dangerous, particularly if there is any spillage. They can, of course, have loose rugs put over them, but these can be a nuisance since they tend to slide and can cause staff and customers to trip. A polished hardwood or parquet floor always looks well in the correct place but it does need a lot of work to keep it looking right. It also tends to be noisy when chairs are drawn out.

Lastly our old friend linoleum: this is perfectly all right in a practical situation such as, say, a transport café or similar establishment. There are also many heavy duty vinyls which have tended to take over from 'lino'. The important thing here is once again to see that its 'weight' is up to the job but, more important, to see that flooring underneath is perfectly flat or you will soon have cracks everywhere. Even the old dodge of putting several copies of your favourite Sunday newspaper between the lino and the boards does not always work.

Lighting

Lighting is always a source of particular interest and its contribution to the overall ambience is considerable. If it is too bright it is not only wasteful of fuel but it also detracts from the relaxing and restful atmosphere that should obtain. Conversely it should not be gloomy and so dark that one cannot read the menu without a flashlight. It should be a carefully considered part of the overall scheme of decoration and character of the whole. One does not expect to find cosy, intimately lit corners in a busy, working-man's café. It is not part of the 'scene' and very often that particular kind of customer will want to read a newspaper comfortably. A restaurant attracting 'popular' trade, which is fast moving, needs fairly bright lighting, whereas the type of establishment where a couple, or a party, may go to spend a pleasant evening requires softer lighting. The form of lighting used greatly influences the mood. The particular arrangement decided upon, therefore, must be complementary to the style of trade, as with the furniture.

Undoubtedly the cheapest form of lighting is the fluorescent tube, but unless it is well diffused and 'warm' white tubes are used, the light is usually hard and garish. It does not have much visual appeal either. Very often the most effective treatment is to conceal the tubes behind cornices, or pelmets, to give a soft and indirect light. Various colours are available to give interest to a scheme, a rose tube giving a very pleasant soft warmth for example. Pot lights inserted into the ceiling and supplemented by wall lights make an attractive combination which is both practical and easy on the eye. Individual table lamps of low wattage always give a feeling of intimacy and luxury. If these are considered, however, in the original planning of the tables, do not forget to specify exactly where you want the electrical points. Whilst the most practical place for these is around the walls of the room, flush-fitting floor points can be fitted but they are often a nuisance in use and destroy the flexibility of centre table movement. They involve trailing flexes which can be a constant source of bother.

The general scheme may well be affected by the height of the ceiling. Being, I hope, an essentially practical person, I will not waste much space on crystal chandeliers. They look beautiful, are enormously expensive and are very difficult to clean and, if you are the kind of restaurateur that is going to install them, I doubt very much if you will be reading this little book for the beginner. Should your ceiling be high try to drop the fittings as low as is practical. Coupled with any of the vast variety of fittings the lighting industry offers today, quite a pleasant scheme can be evolved without undue expense. It is quite a good idea to fit dimmer switches. The lighting can then be at full strength during the day and subdued for the evening business.

Candle-light

Candles always contribute to an authentic atmosphere as long as you do not rely on them for your sole source of lighting. The best kind to buy are the four-hour burning variety such as the Danes excel in manufacturing. They are only a little more expensive initially, but are much cheaper in the long run. The simplest way to deal with them is to put them into bottles such as the Chianti type. If the waste candlegrease is allowed to run over them they will eventually become quite attractive and interesting to look at, particularly if different coloured candles have been used. Otherwise the traditional candelabra in silver or wrought iron is the normal holder. There are quite a number of table lamps, of Scandinavian origin usually, which take the 'night-light' type of candle reminiscent of our extreme youth. These are very cheap, not only to buy but to run as well. Whilst not a genuine candle, a recent innovation on the market is an imitation candle lamp which has a small flickering neon light giving quite a realistic and interesting performance.

Whatever kind of lighting effect you eventually choose, your electrical contractor will advise you best as to what wattage you need consistent with the type of lighting required and the size of the room. It is always worth looking around to get ideas. There is a wealth of fittings on the market but examine them carefully. I sometimes wish those who designed them had to change a lamp bulb occasionally! Match the scheme to the general décor so that it is part of it and does not appear to be an after-thought. If you do install anything which is a little unusual in the way of either glasses, or bulbs themselves, get a few spares or you may be in difficulty for later replacements.

Table Linen

It is sometimes a difficult decision whether to buy one's own linen and napery and launder it, or whether to hire from one of the many companies specialising in this field. If you want to be different, of course, then the chance of getting anything in this category from the hire people is remote. My own feeling is that so long as the standard white cloth is all that you need, then hiring is a good proposition and saves much of the 'house-keeping' problems of not only laundering and repairing, but of constant replacement costs. The need for the thorough check-ing of deliveries and dispatches is no different however. If you lose hired cloths, or other items, you have to pay for them. However, on balance, there is much to be said for the system, particularly in terms of original capital costs.

There is usually a very comprehensive range of items to choose from. Apart from table-cloths and table napkins, it is possible to hire waiters' cloths, glass cloths and tea-cloths, clothing, etc. The table-cloths can be supplied in a large number of sizes from 36in. square to banqueting lengths. Shop around and see what there is to offer, but particularly examine charges as these can vary as well as the conditions attached to the hiring. Do be very thorough in checking everything, particularly shortages in delivery, a note of which should always be made and signed for.

Depending on the volume of trade it will be necessary to decide on the quantity to hire. To start with this cannot be calculated in any other way than by inspired 'guesstimation'. If possible try to arrange your contract on a 'used only' basis until the usage can be fairly accurately gauged. Always keep a supply of smaller size 'slip cloths'. These can be slipped over an existing larger cloth which perhaps has the odd small gravy stain on it. A 36in. cloth is cheaper to hire than a 54in. one! This will enable you to carry a stock and pay for it as you use it. Not many companies are willing to do this and prefer to operate on a fixed quantity per week which means that you have to carry sufficient all the time to cover you at peak trading periods and pay for them whether you use them or not when slack. It is customary, however, to carry three week's supply, one in the laundry, one in use and a spare. This does give some sort of safety valve. It is also possible to 'boost' for a peak period if sufficient notice is given.

Serviettes

Most self-respecting restaurants will supply their customers with a serviette or a napkin. If you intend to operate a really high-class establishment then almost certainly a linen napkin is expected. Paper serviettes however are quite acceptable in normal circumstances and these are available in many thicknesses and sizes. A white single ply 13in. (or 33cm) will be acceptable in a fast food restaurant and, for slightly better class trade, 17in. (43cm) two, or three ply, serviettes. These are sold in a range of several colours and it is usually possible to choose one which suits the décor. Keep a good stock, as supplies have a habit of drying up occasionally in these days of industrial action. Make a study of one or two of the more simple ways of folding your serviettes as these will give a more professional look to your tables.

Cutlery

Selecting the right sort of cutlery for your trade is important. Nothing looks better, of course, than good silver plate and you may not think you can possibly lay up with anything less if your restaurant is that sort of bracket. It only looks good, however, if it is properly cleaned and kept sparkling. Unless you can be sure of getting this particular chore done, it is more practical to consider stainless steel. There are some particularly attractive and distinctive designs being marketed and of quite high quality. Certainly it is a far more workable proposition, easy to wash or pass through the dishwashing machine, and virtually indestructible. Most designs are offered 'en suite', as with silver plate.

Depending on the menu, make sure you buy sufficient for at least a double lay-up, and more if you can afford it. Double up again on such small items as tea or coffee spoons. No matter what precautions are taken to avoid their loss, they do disappear. It makes one very sad at times but one learns to live with it. It is all the more saddening when the restaurateur is trying to maintain a high standard by providing good quality table appointments. It would be wrong to magnify the problem, for it is not large, but it is worth commenting on, and warning against. It does perhaps influence the decision sometimes as to whether to buy quality or not. I think this decision is more pertinent to the cheaper class of operation where losses of this kind are more predominant. One has to strike the right balance as purchasing spoons and forks which bend easily, or knives which do not cut, are only false economies.

Whilst a rough 'rule of thumb' quantity of at least a double lay-up has been mentioned, it should perhaps be stressed that this would be an absolute working minimum and, depending on the menu offered, requires some qualification. For example if hors d'oeuvre and fish are offered then one customer choosing both would require a double fish knife and fork lay-up although you might decide to use a slightly smaller pair of 'fish eaters', as they are known, for hors d'oeuvre service. In these circumstances, therefore, a considerable overlap of fish cutlery would be needed. The same considerations would apply to say, melon as a first course and a similar lay-up for the sweet. These are merely two examples of the need to consider the quantity of cutlery that the menu dictates and indicates the need to give careful thought to overall requirements.

Glassware

Glassware too is a table furnishing which can add to or detract from the standard of your catering. The needs of the establishment might be quite simple and reduced to toughened glass tumblers or, in the case of licensed trade, quite complex with a very full range of glasses 'en suite'. Glassware is the most vulnerable commodity which is handled by the staff in service. Losses and breakages can be very considerable indeed, most of these occurring in the process of washing up. Thought given to the equipment and the particular method used is therefore worthwhile. The provision of specially designed and fitted trays, for example, which prevent movement of glasses whilst being processed through the machine. There are small machines available for washing glasses in the bar. Whilst it is often done, it is not a good idea to mix crockery and glass and cutlery in a dishwashing machine if it can be avoided. Glasses are delicate things and sometimes not a very practical shape, for example long stemmed hock glasses, tall champagne, etc. These are often better washed by hand. I have deliberately mentioned these practical points before considering style, type and quality of the glassware needed.

If the restaurant is to be exclusive and different, the owner may well feel that table appointments should be in keeping with that policy. Catalogues from glass manufacturers display a large number of designs and there should be no difficulty in choosing the right design for you. If the choice is for a style which is exclusive, check on the position regarding replacements. These can sometimes be difficult and nothing looks worse than a mixture. 'Badging' is of course possible but this does involve ordering specified minimum quantities which might well be more than you could store, apart from the financial outlay. Your own 'logo' or badge gives distinction however and a touch of class. I can never be sure whether it deters the souvenir hunter or encourages him, but I suspect the latter. In which case it might be considered right to charge such losses to advertising!

The most popular and probably the cheapest style of glass for general bar use for spirits, fruit juices or service of wine in the restaurant, is the 'Paris goblet'. This can be purchased in many sizes, the 8 oz. being the most useful for general use, water, gaelic coffees, etc.; the $6\frac{2}{3}$ oz. glass is also just about right as a measure for wine specifically sold 'by the glass', although this is obviously a house policy matter. Other sizes are available. Hock or Moselle glasses with their long elegant stems of either brown or green, always give the authentic and luxurious touch but they are really not very practical and are expensive. A tall champagne, with a shorter stem, is a better proposition if cost is a consideration. It is also quite a useful general purpose wine glass although not really recommended for reds or the better white wines as its shape does not allow the bouquet of the wine to come through, having a smaller surface area than the Paris goblet. Whilst mention has been made of the tall champagne glass, the British who originated the shallow champagne 'saucer' still prefer it.

Sherry, port, liqueur and brandy glasses complete the average restaurant requirement. The most common type of sherry and liqueur glass is the 'Elgin suite'. It gives the illusion of containing at least half as much again as the other popular style, the 'Club optic'. The 'Club' however is useful because it can be used for both sherry and port service. The correct glass for sherry is the 'Copita' which is the traditional shape and assists with giving a 'nose' to the wine. It does, however, suffer from the washing up problems referred to earlier. The traditional brandy glass can be obtained in many sizes and it is a question of personal taste – the largest being perhaps rather ostentatious and not very practical. Still on the subject of glass, oil and vinegar bottles, water jugs and ash-trays will be required. Make sure you have plenty of the latter. They often require changing during the course of the meal. Carafes too are needed if you intend to offer a 'house wine' in this way. Since legislation is highly likely to specify in the future the unit quantity sold, it would be wise to ensure that these are litres or half litres.

Crockery

The choice of crockery is yet a further consideration. Without being clumsy, it should be heavy enough to stand up to busy service, vitrified china being the most suitable for catering use.

It will have to withstand a great deal of handling and heat in the kitchen and service hotplates, the dining room and the wash-up. Like the glassware quite a number of designs are obtainable and, again, it is possible to order a specified quantity to be 'badged' or with the restaurant's name on it.

Whilst 'stacking' designs are often not the most elegant and therefore not always suitable for high-class trade, they do have a very great deal to commend them. It is particularly useful to be able to stack cups that nest into each other in a sideboard or on a shelf. They not only take up less space, but are less vulnerable to breakages as well, being easier to carry when stocking up sideboards for service or clearing when dirty. The same applies to soup bowls. Whilst sometimes of smaller capacity, coffee cups can double for tea cups, in which case a demi-tasse would perhaps be required for coffee, particularly for functions.

The normal plate sizes are as follows: side plates $6\frac{1}{2}$in. diameter; fish course, entrée and sweet plates $8\frac{1}{2}$in. diameter (some kinds of first course such as Smoked Trout, etc. can also be served on this latter size); main course plates $9\frac{1}{2}$in. diameter. Should you serve steaks and other grills it is both fashionable and practical to use an 11in. oval dish. An even larger size of 12in. oval is needed for T-bone steaks and Dover Soles. The service of soup can either be by 9in. soup plate or, as is often customary these days, in a bowl. If you want to be really distinctive then an eared 'marmite' with a lid removed at the table makes a nice touch. Sauce boats are usually available in matching pattern but, in practice, a stainless steel article usually looks well and lasts a lifetime. Butter dishes will be needed to complete normal china requirements although ash-trays can likewise be had to match, if preferred to glass.

Condiments

Condiment sets are available in all kinds of materials from cheap plastics to glass, stainless steel, pottery, silver plate and wood. Once again it depends on your trade and there are plenty of styles and types to choose from. The practical point to look for whatever kind you decide on is ease of refilling. Some are notoriously tedious with fine screw threads which clog with salt; others with a 'pea-size' hole through which to pour the salt or pepper and often with a small rubber or cork stopper, which gets lost very quickly. Examine them carefully and imagine yourself with the job of daily refill. The more gimmicky they are then usually the more impractical they are too. In addition to the normal salt, pepper and mustard pot, it may be necessary to have pepper pots for cayenne. If this is so then I suggest you keep these in glass type pots so that the contents are visible to avoid mistakes. A diner can easily ruin his meal otherwise, as well as the staff not knowing which is white or red pepper.

No good class restaurant should be without peppermills. These are usually made of wood and are available in sizes varying from the sublime to the ridiculous! The very large type may add an air of mystique when used by the waiter for his flambé work, but look quite silly when offered to a customer. For table use a peppermill 6in. high is amply large enough and easy to handle. Whilst it is nice to have special stone jars for French mustard, the usual thing is to purchase an original consignment of a sufficient number and then refill them from bulk supplies. Just one small word of caution here. If one particular manufacturer's name is on the jar and you refill with another, you could be in trouble – you do not know who your customers are sometimes! Tabasco sauce is sold in very small bottles which are quite acceptable at the table. On the subject of sauces generally, these should always be of good quality and in 9 oz. approximately sizes and kept on the side-board. A large bottle of chop sauce may be all right on a Hot Dog stand but does not look quite right in a good restaurant. Neither does it commend the food!

Sugars

Sugar basins can either be of stainless steel, or pottery, or of course of silver plate. You will need sufficient for not only cubed sugar but, if your trade is largely coffee in a popular operation, for brown and rock sugar too. Sugar casters or sifters for caster sugar are needed for service of melon, fruit pies, etc. The glass type with a screw top is the most practical. Make sure they are kept dry.

Coupes

Coupes in some form or another feature on most menus. Jacobean glass is the cheapest initially but stainless steel is the most practical. If silver plate however is the theme it would be wrong to mix. Stemmed coupes of silver plate often finish up bent and dented and are not always the best of advertisements. The same applies to Banana Split dishes which are always best in stainless steel, as the glass variety are usually very thick and clumsy and difficult to stack. They are also obtainable in plastic, however, and these are quite acceptable in the popular café style of business. Make sure they do not get near to any heat however.

Tea and Coffee Service

Tea-pots will be required for one, two or four persons and in capacities of $\frac{1}{2}$ pint, 1 pint and $1\frac{1}{2}$ pints. Hot water jugs to match in the same sizes. Jugs for milk in $\frac{1}{4}$ and $\frac{1}{2}$ pint. If in china or pottery they will be of the same design as the other crockery. If purchased in stainless steel, however, or in plate, see that the design of the handle is such that it keeps cool. This is usually effected by a double handle when made of stainless steel, or perforations when of silver plate. If otherwise, it can cause considerable discomfort and frustration to the customer. It is, of course, usual to serve the tea on a tray. The best type is of laminated wood as they keep cooler and are not so noisy in operation.

The most popular method of coffee making today is by the 'Cona' or 'pour-on' method. Service is then effected by pouring the coffee straight from the glass or stainless steel flask. In conjunction with this it is customary to serve a tot of cream, usually in a china or stainless steel $1\frac{1}{2}$ or 2 oz. 'tot'. If, however, you intend to use a more orthodox service you will need coffee-pots of $\frac{1}{2}$ pint and 1 pint capacity with matching jugs or pots of similar size for hot milk. In the latter case the coffee and milk would be dispensed from a 'Café set' in the still-room.

Miscellaneous equipment

Quite a lot of miscellaneous equipment may yet be needed

according to the style of business done. Butane gas or methy-
lated spirit lamps and chafing dishes for flambé work for
example; also trolleys for service at the table side for either
hors d'oeuvre, for filleting fish and other work, or for sweets
and liqueurs. Such equipment is specialist by nature and often
purpose made and designed. It can be simple or complicated.
One can manage with a basic two-tier trolley for example for
most things but the appearance of a chromed rotating hors
d'oeuvre trolley, or one specially fitted for service of liqueurs,
all help to create an authentic and professional atmosphere.
They are usually more efficient in operation too since they are
purpose made for the job. Other special items would include
finger bowls, lobster picks and crackers, dishes for snails,
gâteau slices, grape scissors, crumb scoops, bread boats or
baskets, cheese boards and knives, pastry forks and of course
flower vases. The list is almost endless, the complication increasing with the climb up the social scale.

Wine Storage

Should the restaurant be licensed, and at once it becomes a
more profitable operation because of the type of trade it will
attract, then the storage of wines in the restaurant is a further
consideration. It is not proposed to write a treatise on the
subject of wines since enough exhaustive publications already
exist. However, a few words on the very necessary question of
storage and presentation may not come amiss at this stage.

Red wines are normally served at room temperature and
white and rosé wines are best served chilled. They should be
stored on their side so that the cork does not dry out and
shrink, thus allowing air in. With these simple guidelines in
mind, therefore, it is necessary to rack in 'bins' so that they are
readily identified for service. A suitable corner of the restaurant
can be used to rack the 'reds' where they will not only be
readily available for service and be stored at the correct temperature but make an interesting display feature. It all helps
to give atmosphere. The reserve stocks can be kept in the
cellar or store and only a number, consistent with service requirements, kept in the restaurant. One sometimes sees red
wines stored upright on a shelf. This is a bad practice for the

reasons already explained.

The ideal way to keep white or rosé wines cool is to install a purpose-made cabinet, properly refrigerated. If a white wine is at all warm it takes quite a while to get the temperature down in an ice bucket. Shock treatment to any kind of wine is bad. Examples of this are putting white or rosé wines in a deep-freeze or red wines in the service hotplate. Such treatment can drastically alter the character of the wine and is to be deplored. Far better to explain to the customer. More often than not he will appreciate it.

Wine Cooling

Wine cooling buckets and stands will be required for the service of white or rosé wines and, of course, for sparkling wines. If you are a good enough client, you may be able to approach your supplier for some free. These will probably bear some advertising identity but it is usually in good taste. The same applies to baskets in either half or whole bottle size and used for the service of red wine. You may feel it unnecessary to have cooling buckets for service if you have gone to the expense of a refrigerated cabinet. To some extent this is true but it is still appropriate to use a bucket so that the wine is kept chilled and to preserve the quality appearance of the service.

Unfortunately this is not the end of the matter since it is no good taking chilled wine and plunging it into water which may be several degrees warmer. Ice is required. The most convenient way to produce ice cubes both for bar use and for the wine coolers is to install an ice-making machine. A comparatively small model can produce about 40 lb of ice per day. This is sufficient for the average restaurant. There are very many models on the market. They can be notoriously unreliable and unnecessarily complicated, as well as being easily damaged by misuse. Thoroughly examine and assess practicabilities before you buy. The more simple and rugged the better. Give careful thought too to the installation position which should be near enough to the service requirement but preferably not in the restaurant itself. Such machines need water supply and drainage. If the machine should give trouble you may have a soaked carpet unless precautions are taken when installing. There is also a minor noise problem to consider.

Corkscrews

There are three main types to choose from. The kind used by most wine waiters is known as a 'waiter's friend'. It has a side lever action and is also equipped with a knife blade for removing the top foil round the ridge of the bottle before extracting the cork. In addition some models have a crown cork remover at one end. Because of their single lever side action they require perhaps a little more expertise in use. There is a double lever action cork remover on the market which is widely used and easier to handle. It does necessitate the use of a separate knife however. The third type is that which is more commonly found in households, a corkscrew with a T-handle. The unfortunate tendency is for the bottle to be placed between the knees when opening the bottle. Not a form of practice to be recommended in a professional situation! There is a fourth type of cork remover and operated by a CO_2 gas capsule, but again not recommended for commercial use for a variety of reasons.

Reception and Cash

Both reception and cash can operate from the same point unless organisational requirements dictate otherwise. In a small situation both functions will probably be in the hands of the proprietor or someone of authority. The logical and strategical place for the cash desk, and reception point where bookings are handled, is at the restaurant entrance, for obvious reasons. The bookings sheet, plan or diary, will be needed there when clients arrive and, unless cash is taken at the table, they will be required to pay as they leave. The desk should be equipped with the telephone so that business can be conducted without having to leave the desk. If credit card business is done then a drawer should be provided in which to carry the necessary forms and vouchers as well as the machines for processing the transaction. The cash desk is also a very convenient point from which to effect cigarette sales as it gives better control.

If the trade is licensed a multi-total cash register is useful as one can then isolate food sales from liquor which is necessary in order to ascertain profit percentages later on. Another useful thing is to have posted a list of current foreign currency exchange values if travellers' cheques are to be accepted for example. Spikes will be needed for bill copies. A further lockable drawer should be provided in which to keep a sufficient supply of change.

CHAPTER 5

Restaurant Staffing, Operation and Routine

Staff Attitudes

Having considered, in general terms, the way in which the dining room should be most effectively laid out, and the equipment needed according to the type of operation, we can now proceed a stage further with working routine. It would, however, be pertinent to look at the very important role that is played by staff who have constant contact with the customers such as the waiter or waitress, and even yourself, if you are a 'front man'. You have probably invested several thousands of pounds in your new venture and, having done so, it would not be natural if you did not want to succeed!

The importance of making a customer feel welcome, wanted and looked after, from the moment he enters the door, cannot be over emphasised. Quite obviously the approach must of necessity vary with the class of trade but even in a popular, fast food situation a smile and a bright word of welcome costs nothing and immediately sets the scene. We are a 'hospitality industry' looking after people who are away from their home environment. Once welcomed appropriately it then becomes a matter of discretion and intuition as to whether they are best left quietly alone or otherwise. In the main, people do not like to be fussed, but there are others who expect a great deal of attention and to be the centre of attraction. Experienced staff soon get to recognise the 'type' and react accordingly.

Selection

Obtaining the right staff is not easy; selection is important. Experience has taught me that it is often better nowadays to engage prospective service staff more for their character and personality than for their reputed expertise. As long as the system of work is not too technical and offers only 'plated' service, then it does not usually take more than a few days of sound induction and on-the-job training for a reasonably intelligent person to adapt. Even 'silver service' can be taught and picked up fairly quickly at times. Initially, the qualities to look for are clean, neat personal appearance, good speech and pleasant manner, and above all a good record of health. Whilst circumstances can be fairly desperate and pressurized on occasions it is never good policy to throw new staff in the 'deep end', whether experienced or not. It usually has a nasty boomerang effect. Even 'old hands' need a few days to settle in, learn the system you are operating and ascertain where everything is. More and more the industry is realising the importance of good induction training, particularly as we have to take a growing percentage of staff who are untrained.

As far as service staff are concerned, training can be divided into two main categories. What are termed the 'social skills', and the 'technical skills'. In simple terms the former concerns the ability to make the customer feel welcome and to ensure his personal comfort, and the latter the development of technical ability. The Hotel and Catering Industry Training Board, Ramsey House, Central Square, Wembley, Middlesex, offers an excellent and reasonably priced training package which will assist you to develop the techniques of training new service staff. Another publication which has been used since 1947 by technical colleges as a textbook, and almost a Bible, is *The Waiter** published by Hutchinson and written by John Fuller and A. J. Currie. Either or both of these will be of considerable use and benefit. To return to the original theme,

*Now published as *Modern Restaurant Service* (Hutchinson 1982).

remember that warm and friendly, but not too effusive, greet-
ing. If staff can remember the customer's name it helps
enormously. If they can remember his idiosyncrasies you are
home and dry! This advice goes in full measure whether you
run a 'char and wad' café or a 'restaurant française'. Most of
us like to be flattered, it is one of our human failings; being
remembered is one of the nicest forms of flattery.

Cleaning Routine (Evening)

When business has ceased for the day there is a certain amount
of systematic clearing up to be done in anticipation of getting
the restaurant ready for service next morning. Care should be
taken to see that scraps of food, bread, etc., are not left about
which might encourage vermin. Tables should be cleared and
cloths removed. Since the condiments will have to be refilled,
these should all be placed on a table at a convenient place near
the service. The mustards should be emptied out and the pots
preferably left to soak overnight. It is often possible to re-use
the mustard, particularly if it is of the 'ready-mixed' variety.
A thin skin of water, or vinegar over the surface will effectively
prevent a crust forming. The dining chairs should be placed
upside down with their seats on the table tops. This will enable
the carpet or floor to be cleaned next morning without obstruc-
tion. Flowers, if any, should be removed and placed in a pail
of fresh water. They will then recuperate overnight and be
ready for rearranging. It is always good policy to cash up the
till. It is then easier to sort out discrepancies than left until
next day. Never leave the till locked overnight but leave the
drawer open. Should you be unfortunate enough to be burgled,
the thieves could do a great deal of expensive damage in
forcing the till drawer open only to find nothing there. Check
all security thoroughly such as windows and doors. Ensure
that ash-trays are emptied safely and no smouldering cigarette
ends left about.

Morning Routine

Traditionally, service staff are responsible for cleaning, putting
the vacuum cleaner over the carpet, dusting and polishing in

addition to cleaning the silver, etc. You may find it more convenient to engage a cleaner to arrive earlier to do the more menial tasks and give the restaurant a good 'airing'. This will allow the service staff to arrive later and concentrate on getting everything in readiness for service. This process is known as getting 'mise en place' done. Literally this means 'making in place' and covers a multiplicity of routine tasks, all of which have to be carried out daily under the eye of the head waiter or restaurant supervisor before the first customer can be served.

Such tasks involve stocking up the stations or sideboards with cleaned and polished cutlery, tea cups and saucers, coffee cups and saucers, side plates, etc. Sauce boats are filled with Tartare Sauce, Mint Sauce, Horseradish and perhaps Vinaigrette. The condiment sets will need refilling with salt, pepper and mustard; peppermills to be topped up with black or white pepper corns. Bottles are refilled with vinegar and olive oil. Bread baskets or boats are stocked with fresh rolls. There is much to do and it will be necessary for a work rota to be arranged in order that an equitable system is worked.

Laying-up

Glass and cutlery always require a final polish before being laid, however well they have been washed. Cutlery which is of silver plate requires special attention as forks, particularly, get black between the prongs if they have been used for eggs or have had contact with acids such as vinegar. Even stainless steel requires a good polish or it will look dull. Depending on your style of operation you may or may not wish to lay up tables ready for business. It is customary to lay up with basic cutlery and glass requirements in a good class house. The only drawback sometimes is that cutlery or glasses may have to be changed, i.e. fish cutlery instead of meat knife and fork, hock glasses instead of Paris goblets, etc. This is simply done after the order has been taken and it is, in any case, less time-consuming than putting down a full lay-up. The fish cutlery should then be taken to the table on a serviette on a salver or plate, never carried loose in the hands. Fresh table-cloths will have to be laid, or if the original table-cloths are only lightly soiled, a smaller 'slipper cloth' placed over the top diagonally. This, if you remember, helps the laundry or hire-cost situation. When each group of tables or 'station' has been laid up the tables should be checked for correctness and cleanliness by the person in charge. Details do get missed and it is annoying if the client has to ask for an ash-tray as soon as he has been seated and more so if he has to tell you that the salt cellar is empty.

Menus and Wine Lists

The first thing a customer is handed after being seated is the menu, and possibly the wine list if there is not a wine waiter. First impressions are important and a dirty, torn or gravy-stained menu will not help in giving the right one. You will have your own views on what form the actual dimensions and menu cover will take. Some restaurants offer a menu cover as large as a Sunday newspaper which I personally think is ostentatious and not very practical. However, it is a matter of personal opinion. The ideal size to handle is about 10in. by 8in. Covers do help to keep the menus clean and they can be wiped over each day prior to service. As the à la carte menu is a fairly permanent list, it does not have to be disturbed except for occasional changes of dishes and price structure. If a daily table d'hôte is offered this will be either hand written (which appeals to the purists) or typed. It is a good idea to keep this loose or clipped to the inner page, or pages, as the clear acetate sheeting soon gets torn and tatty in appearance if handled too frequently.

There are several manufacturers who will make up menu covers to your personal requirements offering a choice of colour, sizes, inner pages or pockets and with whatever details, name, etc., you require on the outside.

Wine lists can, of course, be treated in the same way as the menus with cards inside a purpose-made cover or with inner pockets to take more than two cards, which would probably be the case. Have them made in a different colour or size and titled so that they are easily distinguished from the menu and thus avoid errors when presenting them at the table. A wine merchant will quite often undertake to bear the printing costs and provide an attractive 'glazed' cover free if your business interests them. Try them out. The only trouble here sometimes is that it tends to tie you since they will expect you to list a certain number of their wines, and you may also want to replace the covers through wear and tear; you might then experience difficulty in obtaining more. The best arrangement is to have your own permanent covers made and get the merchant to pay for the printing of loose cards, or even the covers themselves initially. It will depend on how much you are spending with them!

However you decide to make arrangements for the provision of your menus and wine lists, do see that a plain bold form of type-face is used. Customers do like to be able to read them comfortably, particularly if your lighting is at all subdued. If you should list French or other foreign classical dishes, a short description of the style and garnish etc., in English, helps the customer and creates interest. It does not have to be lengthy but sufficient to indicate, say, 'poached in white wine with mushrooms and shallots' for example. Wine lists can contain outline maps of the district of origin and a few relevant facts. If you do make any statements though, do see that they are accurate.

Unless the menu is simple and a single page that can be conveniently placed in a clip on the table, the menus (and wine lists) are conveniently kept on the station sideboard for presentation after seating, or alternatively at the reception so that they can be picked up and handed to the customer after they are shown to their table.

Table Numbers

The numbering of tables is primarily of interest to the staff in allocation of stations and in order to deal with bookings on the 'plan'. I am never quite sure what practical purpose is served otherwise in having a number visible to the customer unless subsequent identification is needed for reference. You might be asked for say 'Table 14, where I sat last time' – perhaps six months previously. In this respect it could be useful, but table numbers are notoriously attractive to souvenir hunters. Fortunately they are usually of plastic or perspex, and easily replaceable from most catering suppliers fairly cheaply.

Bookings

Booked tables are a mixed blessings but almost inevitable in better class trade. A 'mixed blessing' because they introduce a certain amount of inflexibility until you approach a position where almost all the seating is booked over perhaps two or three sittings. You then arrive happily at a situation where you are in the position to dictate and plan your seating. Always try to avoid the room filling up totally at any one particular time. If this is allowed to happen it throws a very heavy load on the kitchen if the menu is all à la carte and results in bad service and periods of waiting at the table while the mixed orders are processed. If you can possibly do so, stagger the booking times on each station. This will ensure a fairly full and even flow of orders to the kitchen thus avoiding rush periods to some degree. Should you have a sizeable party booked, try to avoid taking bookings at the same time unless you are sure your organisation can cope with it.

The booking sheets or plans can be evolved in any form that suits you as long as it is easy to identify and clear in its purpose. One way is to reproduce on a stencil a plan of the room and write in spaces for names and times on each table. You can then run off as many copies as you want and keep them on a clip board in reception. The important thing is to ensure that, whatever system you choose to operate, any possibility of a double booking is eradicted. Avoid undue complication and keep the plan as simple as possible.

Another method is to rule off sheets of foolscap with columns for name, time and table number or with separate squares for each table. As long as you devise a foolproof system it does not really matter. Should you wish to turn the tables over two or three times, then it is necessary from experience to know how long you can afford to let a table be occupied. The higher the class of trade and the more elaborate the service, the longer the table will be required – perhaps all evening. On the other hand you may find from experience that two hours is about right or, of course, even less. If you operate a fast food outlet then half an hour might well be the average and in these circumstances bookings should not interest you and would be a positive encumbrance. So much depends on your style of operation as to whether you consider it necessary or wise to maintain a policy of booked tables.

One last word of caution on this subject however. If it is at all possible, restrict the authority to accept bookings to as few staff as possible, preferably only one or two people. This will considerably reduce the possibility of errors. The system of back-up administration for larger parties and functions will be dealt with in a later chapter.

Taking the order – The Order Pad

Whilst we are not strictly concerned at this juncture with control systems, some reference should be made to the way the customer's order is to be recorded and dealt with. Quite a number of differing ways of processing the order are operated in various establishments; these are often tailored and designed to meet the needs of the proprietor and the style of work. In a simple café with a very limited and simple menu handling a small number of customers, the spoken word is probably sufficient across the service counter. Once however the slightest degree of complication or business pressure enters the scene then some written record becomes essential.

The order serves two main purposes initially. The waitress, or waiter, has a record and the kitchen is informed exactly what dishes are required. The waiter has an 'aide-memoire' to which to refer in selecting what particular cutlery, or accompaniments, etc., are wanted and also evidence on which to base the bill. The kitchen knows how the customer requires the dishes cooked and garnished and in what number and sequence. Various styles of kitchen order pads are available and they vary in complexity. Certainly the waiter will need a copy of the order from which to work after he has deposited the kitchen copy. A standard type of pad, therefore, has tear-off sections and a carbon back. It also has a large identifying waiter's number which can be torn off and used to identify finished dishes on the service hotplate. The leaves of the pad also have serial numbers which subsequently assist control.

Some variations of this particular style of pad also incorporates a third copy which forms the customer's bill. This, however, only lends itself to a simple style of operation. A complicated, mixed à la carte order usually contains far too much varied information and a separate pad is required for the final making up of the bill. This can be of a standard type or specially printed according to requirements. Both the kitchen order pad and the bill pad can be housed in a cover designed for the purpose, the pads being held in with crocodile clips.

Writing the Order

There is always a temptation for the waiter to use abbreviations for names of dishes, particularly when under pressure. This is quite in order as long as the chef knows exactly what is meant and a standard form of abbreviation is used. The order should be written with clarity. Failure to do this usually means mistakes, with the customer not getting what he ordered, or wasted food when the order is rectified, wasted time and a dissatisfied client.

The table number should be written on the order. It is usual to take the order for the first course and the main course (or fish course) at the same time. This allows the kitchen to deal with the main course while the customer is eating whatever he has chosen to start with. Care should be taken to enquire how the customer requires his steak cooked, if these are served. Blue, rare, medium rare, medium or well done. With any meat that requires only a little cooking, it is useful if the grill cook can be given an indication as to the progress of the first course. This will enable him to cook the meat at precisely the right moment thus ensuring perfection. When actually taking the order from the client it is better to take the first and main course together rather than dealing with all the starters first and then going round the table again for main course orders. This forms a more logical link in the waiter's mind and helps him remember when referring back to his pad as to each customer's sequence of food. The other way of course is to deal with each diner in rotation, ladies first, from a fixed point. When the dishes arrive at the table he will then know in which order to put them down or deal with them from the sideboard or wagon. When under pressure it is surprising how difficult it is sometimes to remember. A system is very necessary.

It is then customary to deal with sweet or cheese orders when the main course plates have been cleared. The wine, or drink order (but not liqueurs), will be taken when first and main course orders have been decided on. According to the dishes selected, the client will then be able to decide on a suitable wine or wines to accompany the meal.

The food order having been dispatched to the kitchen the waiter can then deposit a chit for the wine and make it ready for service. If it is one which requires chilling it will be placed in an ice bucket or, if a red, in a wine basket. The wine can then be presented to the customer in order that it can be verified as correct with regard to type and vintage, if any. Once the wine has been satisfactorily presented it can then be opened. This is particularly necessary where red wines are concerned as it gives them a chance to 'breathe' before being poured.

Having cleared the first course plates away, the host is offered 'a taster' so that he may be assured that the wine is in correct condition for his guests. Whilst it does not often happen, a wine may prove to be 'corky' or out of condition. The experienced waiter will have sniffed the cork on opening to check for this and thus avoid embarrassment at the table. Wines which are not in good condition will usually give off a slight mustiness and probably be dull and cloudy as well as being acid perhaps. Some wines, particular reds of good age, will throw a sediment. Care must be taken when handling such wines to be gentle and avoid undue movement, and also not to serve from the bottom of the bottle. Red wines should be opened whilst still in the basket or cradle. It is not usual to decant precious vintage red wines in a restaurant unless the customer has perhaps produced them himself and has requested it. In such cases the restaurant will invariably make a 'corkage' charge. Prior to the service of coffee the wine list can be presented again for choice of liqueurs.

Presentation of the Bill

According to the system adopted, the bill should be progressively made up and the information taken from the order carbon. If a 'cover charge' is levied this will embrace such items as rolls and butter. If no such charge is made then care must be taken to ensure that such items do not get overlooked. A note should be made on the order pad when service of such sundries is made. Normally in a good-class restaurant the bill is not presented until requested, when it should be all ready to be totalled. Circumstances may require that the table is needed for a subsequent booking, in which case diplomacy should be exercised when presenting the bill. In a popular, or fast food operation, there is not so much need of decorum and it is ordinarily expected that the bill will be presented at once, usually with the coffee or as soon as the meal is eaten. Either way it is customary to fold the bill so that the total is not visible to the guests, if any, and to present it on a side plate to the host should there be one. The customer should always be sent on his way with a pleasantry, a courteous thank you and a smile – regardless of gratuities!

Service Charge

Forgetting the principles of distribution, let us consider the desirability or otherwise of levying a service charge, or whether to leave the giving of the gratuity to the client if he feels so disposed. There are, of course, many points of view depending on which side of the fence you are!

The giving and receiving of gratuities are traditional in the industry. The 'service charge' is a recognition of this and is operated nearly all over the world. It is viewed in many ways; at worst as a supplement to the wages and income of the staff. Trade union thinking would indicate a desire for its abolition and suggest higher wages in its place. Another school of thought is that it avoids the customer having to concern himself as to the level of tip he should leave. However, some clients even tip on top of the service charge on occasions. Further considerations are how the service charge should be distributed and to whom and on what basis.

If we accept the principle that a gratuity, whether added to the bill as a charge, or given otherwise voluntarily, is a reward and an appreciation of service given, it may be contrary to the wishes of the customer that others besides the members of staff who rendered the service should receive part of it. It is a fact that where no service charge is levied and tipping is left to the customer, some staff do much better than others. This is because they give a more attentive service and go out of their way to ensure the success of the meal. The gratuity then becomes an incentive. Conversely staff who do not perhaps work as hard or are not as pleasant to their customers receive a share from the efforts of their colleagues. The incentive aspect is gone. The arguments are interminable! Perhaps it is time that there should be a change but I doubt if you will ever stop tipping in some form or another. Some customers tip in genuine appreciation, some because they want to be remembered, some do not tip at all. It is a subject which is both boring and interesting at the same time.

The operation of the 'tronc', as the cumulative service charge is known, has been a thorn in the side of the industry for years. Personally I prefer to leave it to the customers. You may feel that the system of the service charge is more equitable, and in some ways it is. Too many extras on the bill such as Value Added Tax, service charge, cover charge, and sometimes an 'entertainment' charge, tend to shock the customer when the bill is presented. It is a policy decision which only you can decide in the light of your style of business and your personal views.

Cover Charge

Perhaps a further word is necessary on the question of a 'cover charge'. Nowadays the levying of a cover charge is only made in higher class establishments and is a legacy from the Edwardian period when an additional charge was made to cover napery and other table appointments, rolls and butter and even coffee in some cases. Again it is a policy matter. It does not help goodwill if it proves to be a bit of a 'con' however. Should such a charge be made it should be clearly stated on the menu together with other extras, such as V.A.T. as well as any 'minimum charge'.

CHAPTER 6

Control, Records and Accounts

What Control Means

When applied in relation to the small business, the word 'control' at first sounds rather grand and unnecessary. Controlling can, of course, be an elaborate system of cross checking and statistics-keeping requiring quite a large amount of work and time-consuming effort. Conversely, it can be reasonably simple. As long as the system adopted justifies itself in terms of running the business efficiently, so that profitability can be easily identified and wastage and losses prevented, that is the main object. In simple terms, the bigger the cash flow, number of customers served, quantities of goods handled and staff employed, then the greater is the need for control. Even in a small one-man business a certain amount of paperwork must be done if the enterprise is to be successful.

Small operators are very often hard-working, practical people who find themselves with little time to spare for paperwork and who loathe it anyway. How often does one hear the words 'Oh, I leave all that to my accountant.'? By the time the accountant receives the books, if any, for audit, it may be too late to rectify a loss. A business must be run in a business-like way and the owner should know, at any time, his margins of profitability. This is particularly vital in periods of rapidly spiralling costs. It can only be effected by efficient record-keeping so that, at the least, a monthly analysis of assets, consumption and revenue reflecting ultimate profitability is a known and recognisable fact.

In short, control means employing a system of paperwork which gives information to the restaurateur, or caterer, which can identify areas of profit and loss, record purchases and their correct use through proper stock-keeping, and protect assets. Carelessness in any of these areas could result in cash, or goods, or both, being misappropriated without detection; in sales not yielding the necessary profit margins, or any at all; even in the fact that the proprietor is 'drawing' money in excess of what the business can afford! To try to run a business with just a cheque book stub is not on. It is the first step down the slippery slope. If the caterer is not prepared to carry out some form of control, however basic, he will have forfeited any chance of success financially, although perhaps he might well have achieved it gastronomically. Targets must be set and results compared. Corrective action, if needed, must be taken.

Areas of Control

Control is one thing. What we shall call back-up statistics is another. In a small business control means safeguarding assets; to simplify, that is, cash and stocks. It is true of course that silver and other equipment certainly come into the category of assets. They have to be bought initially and replaced out of profits if they go astray. However, where the small café/ restaurant business is concerned it is accountability for cash, the check system used, and the purchasing, storing and issuing, as well as the correct, economic and proper use of liquor and food stocks that are of prime importance.

Check System Employed

At worst, a verbal order can be taken from a customer, given to the kitchen, served, the customer told the amount of the sale and the cash collected by the waitress. No paperwork at all! This might be perfectly sound if the business is very small and the proprietor's wife is the waitress and the proprietor himself is the chef; they are hardly likely to cheat themselves.

Disregarding any inefficiency that such lack of paperwork would contribute to under pressure, such as forgotten items etc., once staff are employed a completely clear field is opened up to encourage fraud. There is no check against food consumption and dishes sold. A considerable proportion of the meat stock could go out of the back door for example without detection. The waitress could easily make a nice little pile on the side without checks and duplicate bills to provide comparison records. Worse still if she is allowed access to the till. She might only ring up part of the amount, or none at all. So there is no check against cash taken and revenue.

A good system of check operation must, therefore, be introduced as a measure of protection. Not that all check systems are fraud proof by a long way. I once worked at a famous London hotel where the waiter would give the larder chef a check for a beef sandwich, receive a caviar sandwich (or smoked salmon) worth a considerably higher selling price, take cash for the caviar sandwich and only pay for the cheaper beef sandwich. The waiter and the larder chef then split the difference. This was, to some extent, possible because the customer paid the waiter and not the cashier. When this racket was caught up with by the advent of a new 'controller' joining the company, customers thereafter had to pay the cashier. This is only one example of possible loopholes; the opportunities for fiddling in the catering industry are legion. A sound check system can at least do much to eliminate the risks as long as the system is carried right through to final office checking. The system adopted should be made to fit the business, not the business made to suit the system. Therefore, devise what is necessary for your particular operation.

As we have briefly seen in the preceding chapters, the check is a source of information to the kitchen for purposes of service. It is also a source of information to the office as a check on the number of customers/dishes served. The waiter/waitress has a copy of the order from which to make up the bill. The customer's bill should also have a carbon copy. When the bill has been paid, both the copy of the order and the bill should be spiked together. If the cash register has a till roll it is then possible to check each transaction and 'ringing up' against the spiked order and bill carbon copies, and against the waitress or waitresses books. Apart from the instance of wrong change-giving, should the till be 'down', it is possible to go back over the spiked bills and check against the till roll. Since both order pads and bills are consecutively numbered this will give a further check against any particular number of staff. Any missing bill can be questioned. It depends how far you wish to go, or indeed, have time to go. The carbon copy of the bill can be checked arithmetically to see if errors in addition have been made. You can then take what action you see fit. The order pad often has the waiter's number in large heavy type for identification purposes. This can then be used as a further check on the number of covers he or she has served and the cash taken.

All this procedure sounds tedious perhaps but the very fact that there is evidence of control being carried out is at least a deterrent to fraudulent activities. Spot checks can be made at intervals and once staff know that this is happening it will induce them to take care, particularly if you decide to make them responsible for their losses caused by errors in addition or missed items from bills. It is not, perhaps, a job that has to be done every day. The day's bills can be kept in clips and checked during a quiet period, but to leave it too long would be to nullify the effect. If a cashier is employed she could be responsible for checking the accuracy of bills perhaps but there is a possible collusion weakness here. It is really a function of management or office to implement the control factor. At the end of the day's business, the till roll and the carbons of the orders and bills should be passed to the office. The till will be 'cashed up' and agreed. Any discrepancies should be looked into at once and the cause identified. This is possible with a check system in operation. Without it, it is not. It is also important that checks be given for any wines drawn, or drinks obtained from a dispense bar so that it can be verified that such items were in fact charged for.

Back-Up Statistics

The back-up statistics that the check system provides, being quite apart from fraud prevention, are both useful and essential. The most useful barometer of progress is to know factually the number of covers the business is turning over against a similar period in the previous year. Since all year round average business will usually follow an activity pattern which is surprisingly faithful in its variations, it is rather pointless to compare one month with the one preceding. The annual comparison is more realistic. In a period of inflation, one would hope to see turnover rise if prices have been properly reviewed and increases implemented. The fact that one's turnover may have gone up, say 15 per cent, is therefore not the main issue. What is interesting is whether 15 per cent more covers have been served and what their spending power was. It only takes a few minutes each day to enter in a 'rough book' on a daily basis, with a weekly total, the takings on food, liquor and tobacco, and the number of covers served. If the book is ruled off in such a manner as to cover three, four or five years side by side, it is then possible to monitor progress at a glance. If the takings are divided by the number of covers it is then possible to see what the average spending power per customer has been. This can be done monthly. When Value Added Tax was first introduced it was interesting to note, in my own business, that spending power for the first month or so remained almost the same, despite a built-in ten per cent tax. This meant that my customers were buying cheaper dishes and that, factually, spending power had dropped. Once the public's resistance to the tax weakened, spending power restored itself. I merely mention this, in passing, to illustrate part of the story that keeping a few simple figures can tell. When assessing revenue figures of course the Value Added Tax element should always be isolated and excluded. It assists cash flow but it is not part of the takings of the business.

Working Percentages

The 'trading' or 'gross profit' figure is a vital statistic. Whilst it is possible to work it out weekly I do not personally feel that this is really necessary unless perhaps the operation is serving a mainly table d'hôte menu and the business is very small. If the costings are sound and the kitchen properly run, a monthly check on the gross profit figure should be sufficient. The need, in a licensed restaurant, to keep separate the figures for food sales and those of liquor and tobacco, has been mentioned in connection with the desirability for a multi-total cash register to be installed. If this is not done then it becomes difficult to arrive at true performance figures. The profit margins on liquor and tobacco, particularly on the latter, are much smaller than on food sales. The effect of lumping the two together would be to pull down drastically the food percentage and it would be difficult to see which of the two areas was responsible for a drop in profitability. At the end of the month, therefore, it should be possible to calculate quickly the total sales figure for food and, by dividing the purchases figure into it, to arrive at a gross profit percentage.

Stock Values

One factor, however, has not been taken into account and that is the value of stocks. If the business is very small, and perhaps heavy purchases of dry goods have been made in a particular month, the effect on the percentage could be quite drastic. The proper procedure is to evaluate the food stocks existing at the beginning of the month and add these into the purchases figure. The stock value held at the close of the month should be deducted. If, however, turnover is high and the stock evaluation figure known to be fairly constant it would be fair to disregard this factor and only take it into account half yearly or even annually. Circumstances obviously dictate the need but, for real accuracy, there is no doubt that stocks should be accounted for monthly, although few hard-working restaurateurs will have time to stock-take and evaluate monthly, and in a practical situation they will know the extent of their purchases during the month in question.

The same procedure applies to liquor and tobacco sales receipts and purchases, and a separate percentage figure should be worked out. The resultant percentages should then be compared with the previous month's results and targets. Any drop in profitability will then immediately be seen and corrective action can be taken after carefully analysing the reasons. If, for example, it was a known fact that during the month potatoes, beef, or some such much used commodity, had cost much more and you had not yet adjusted selling prices, the lower percentage could be, to some extent, explained. If, however, commodity prices had remained stable (and ignoring the question of stock levels) the percentage had dropped it could point to one of several things, e.g. food wastage, bad portion control or even misappropriation. The lower liquor percentage could well uncover some fraud or the other, and give warning. Liquor requires much more frequent stock-taking depending on the type of trade, and particularly if you run bars.

Books of Account

The extent to which a small business needs to go in order to keep proper records which will satisfy the proprietor, his accountant and the Inland Revenue, is really a question of need and expediency. The subject of book-keeping worries most small operators and they feel it is something which is totally foreign and quite outside their scope, or that they cannot spare the time for it. The principles of double-entry book-keeping, monthly trial balances, quarterly profit and loss accounts and even the Annual Statement of Accounts and Balance Sheet are often unfortunately beyond the comprehension of the average small restaurateur or café proprietor. 'How much have I made?' is generally all he wants to know when he pays his annual visit to his accountant. Yet, book-keeping need not be so very frightening or difficult. In fact it is something which any businessman or woman can find both absorbing and fascinating. Whilst not so arithmetically foolproof as double-entry, single-entry book-keeping is at least better than nothing, and should be within the ability of most people who wish to run a small business. Many of our larger specialist stationery firms, such as Kalamazoo or Lamson Paragon, produce systems designed for the small operator which are cleverly devised and foolproof. Working on a carbon system, various transactions are recorded simultaneously and simply. Such systems are accepted by Inland Revenue, one type coming to mind being a Wages Record Book which eliminates the use of tax-deduction cards for example. If, after examination of any of the book-keeping systems such as those mentioned, you feel that you have sufficient expertise to devise your own, perhaps in order to provide more detailed analysis, so much the better.

Quite obviously, in one short chapter it is not feasible, or possible, to delve into the realms of accountancy. There are many specialised books to be read on the subject and courses that can be taken. What I will attempt to do is to outline in practical terms those books of account which will provide a reasonably sound basis of operation and record keeping and, at the same time, provide such statistical information as to enable one to monitor profit and loss satisfactorily.

Cash Book (Main Journal)

This 'prime entry' ledger records ultimately every penny which the business spends and receives. It likewise records all banking transactions as well as cash. It does not, however, indicate indebtedness to traders or individuals to whom the business owes money, known as creditors, or monies due to the business from debtors. It is necessary to keep further ledgers to record these particular aspects. The cash book simply shows on the one hand the revenue when it is received, and the expenditure on the other. It can, therefore, show at any time by simple balancing the state of the bank balance, and of the cash in hand. To do this at least four main columns are necessary. The left-hand side of the book will record all money taken in the way of restaurant receipts or from any other source. It should be ruled to take care of both cash and banking transactions (see Figure 1). The right-hand side of the book shows all payments made by cheque to creditors in the banking column and cash payments in the other. It is also customary, and indeed useful, to rule a third column on each side in which a note is made of the purpose of the transaction, usually called a 'narration'.

Further information is needed in the way of receipt numbers, ledger account numbers, etc. A second bank column may be introduced on the expenditure side. For the purposes of simplicity at this stage, however, it may be easier to ignore it and elaborate shortly as we develop our system (see 'Non-Bought Ledger Aspect' below). Our first concern is to illustrate how the two aspects of income and expenditure are dealt with through the medium of the cash book.

The illustration shows typical entries of a simple kind in the cash book and demonstrates both aspects of receipts and payments. Dealing first with the banking aspect, it shows that the figure brought forward was £10,000 on the revenue side. This figure comprises the true opening balance at the beginning of the financial year plus all amounts banked since. To arrive at the current true figure and disregarding unpresented cheques outstanding, the bank figure of £7,375 on the expenditure side must be deducted which would leave a balance of £3,225 after the banking of £600 had been taken into account. This bank figure on the expenditure side of £7,375 would comprise all the payments made by cheque. However, for a figure to be produced which would agree with the bank statement it is necessary to prepare a 'bank reconciliation'. In simple terms this means that the bank will not have knowledge of cheques which have been paid out by the business and have yet to be presented. If for instance these are missing from the bank statement when it is checked and total, say £150, then, if all is correct, the statement would show not £3,225 but £3,375. In other words because the bank shows that you have £X in your account this is not necessarily the true figure. The reconciliation statement should be prepared monthly as a check on the accuracy of both the cash book and, indeed, of the bank itself.

To deal with the cash aspect, the revenue side shows that the restaurant takings were £300 that day. However, a debtor also paid in £175 for an out-standing wedding account making total receipts of £475. The brought forward cash figure of £13,000, which comprises all similar receipts to date and includes the opening cash balance at the beginning of the financial year, is added making a total of £13,475.

The expenditure cash side of the book shows that certain expenses were incurred. Some flowers were bought and the wages paid out were £350. It also shows a contra entry of £600. This latter figure is the cash which was taken out for banking. The brought forward figure of £12,450 comprises all cash expenditure to that date. When the column is totalled and taken from the revenue cash side of the book the resulting balance should equate with the cash left in the safe, floats or cash box. In this instance this would be £72 and would be what is considered a safe amount to hold for change or further envisaged small cash purchases.

Figure 1. EXAMPLE OF CASH BOOK
Revenue

Date		Bank £		Cash £		Narration
	Balance b/fwd	10,000	00	13,000	00	
3.3.75	By takings			300	00	Restaurant
	,, Dr a/c			175	50	Mr Jones
						Wedding
	,, cash to bank	600	00			Contra
	Pencilled totals	10,600	00	13,475	00	

Expenditure

Date	Ledger No.		Receipt No.	Bank £		Cash £		Narration
		Balance b/fwd		7,000	00	12,450	00	
3.3.75	103	Smith & Co.	114	375	00			Ledger a/c
	104	Floral World	115			3	50	Flowers
	105	Net Wages	W/B			350	00	Staff wages
	106	Bank to cash	C			600	00	Contra
				7,375	00	13,403	50	

The cash book therefore records the cash flow position of the business, including Value Added Tax on takings and the expenditure. This information is never quite up to date however since it does not take into account, as we have noted, sundry debtors and creditors. The business may be owed money from functions, credit card companies and other sources, and of course if monthly tradesmen's accounts are being run the business may owe quite an amount of money by the end of the month. The true state of affairs is only revealed when a trial balance or a periodic profit and loss account is effected and finally when the accountant produces his annual statement of accounts.

Bought Ledger Account (Creditors)

Most businesses run monthly credit accounts with suppliers. Each delivery of goods should, indeed must, be accompanied

by an invoice or a delivery note followed by an invoice, showing the fullest details of the purchase, i.e. date, weight, unit
price and Value Added Tax if any. Before the invoices are
entered in the ledger they should be very carefully checked
for arithmetical accuracy. This will reward well in terms of
money savings. It is surprising how often one can be over-
charged and a wrong addition or calculation can add pounds
to the bill. Although this is time consuming and it is easier to
be trusting, it will not be long before you are glad you started
the practice of checking.

A book should be ruled up with columns for the date,
invoice number (your own), details of goods, amount of the
purchase, payments and credits. A suitable number of pages
should be left for each supplier and an index arranged on the
flyleaf of the ledger showing which numbered pages apply. It
is then simply a matter of keeping the relevant page entered
and updated as goods and invoices are delivered. Each invoice
is given a number and kept in a box file for future reference.
At the end of the month when the statement is received from
the supplier it can be checked against the details of invoices
entered through the month and agreed or otherwise. Payment
can subsequently be made if the account is found correct and
a new balance is struck. By adding all the outstanding balances
at the end of the month it is then possible to ascertain the
amount of indebtedness to tradesmen. It is interesting to compare this figure with the bank balance in the cash book. You
might be over purchasing.

Bought Ledger Analysis

It is now logical to proceed one step further since, having
entered our invoices in the bought ledger account book, we
should analyse the purchases under various headings. This
information is important because it breaks down the expenditure and we can start to produce our operational percentages
on food, liquor and of our other working overheads, etc.

A ledger account book is required with as many columns
as are needed for analysis breakdown. After each invoice has
been entered in the bought ledger account the relevant details,
date, invoice number, bought ledger number and amount are

entered in the appropriate column. Thus, at the end of the month, or at any chosen time, the amount spent on provisions for example can be seen. By taking our revenue figure for food (and opening and closing stocks) into account a food profit percentage can be arrived at. Liquor and tobacco figures can be similarly treated.

Non-Bought Ledger Aspect

Earlier reference was made, when dealing with the cash book, to a 'non-bought ledger' aspect and a second bank column being introduced under this heading on the expenditure side. So far we have assumed that all payments made by cheque through the bank column will have been those for which the business has a ledger account. In practice, however, this will not be the case and there will be many payments by cheque to other parties in the same way that cash amounts are paid out. This then is what is meant by the term 'non-bought ledger' There would be nothing wrong in using one bank column for both bought and non-bought ledger items, but this would entail extracting figures when we arrived at a trial balance situation. It is therefore easier and tidier to keep a second bank column as shown.

Non-Bought Ledger Analysis Book

So far, we have only looked at half the picture. In the same way that the details of all ledger account invoices have been entered in the bought ledger analysis book, so are all the details of expenditure, either by cheque or cash, taken from the cash book non-bought ledger columns. Since such purchases are likely to cover a much wider field a larger number of columns will probably be needed, once again depending on the degree of analysis required. There will doubtless be columns for purchasing of provisions, and for liquor and tobacco possibly. It will be necessary to add such totals to those in the bought ledger analysis book in order to compute gross profit percentages. Thus there is a complete breakdown of all expenditure whether it be for wages, thus enabling a wage cost percentage to be worked out, or for gas, electricity and water, advertising, cleaning materials, stationery, telephone and office expenses, etc. Such figures can then be compared with budget targets for example and a great deal of useful statistical information starts to emerge.

Takings Book

To avoid the necessity to extract figures from the cash book it is useful to keep a separate takings book. By this means it is possible to see at any time up-to-date figures. If some aspect of sales is not subject to V.A.T., such as take-away foods at the time of writing, it is necessary to segregate such figures so that tax payable on meals served in the restaurant can be properly and accurately assessed.

Sundry Debtors Ledger

Should the restaurant provide facilities for functions of any kind, wedding receptions, club dinners, dinner dances or credit-card companies perhaps, it is more than likely that payment will be made at a later date. Such accounts are known as sundry debtors, i.e. money that is owed to the business. If this is the case then a further ledger account must be raised. In a later chapter the back-up organisation will be discussed. At this stage, however, we are only concerned with the financial aspect. In the same way that money owing to creditors from the business is recorded, so must amounts due from debtors be similarly treated. The restaurant may be operating a high-class trade offering monthly credit account facilities with clients signing bills or, very often, credit-card agencies. In which case it will be necessary to create an index with specifically numbered pages for each client's account. In other cases a general heading is all that is necessary.

Columns will be needed for the date, brief details of the transaction or name, the amount of the credit, the amount of the debit when paid, discounts in the case of credit cards, and finally one in which to enter the amount of the distributable service charge if any. When the client remits, the amount paid is entered in the debit column together with discounts or service charge and a new balance struck in the case of regular monthly accounts, or written off otherwise. The amount paid is then taken through the cash book into the cash column of the revenue side as it then becomes part of the cash in hand and of the next banking. It is then finally recorded in the takings book. It is not entered in this latter book until it is paid for the simple reason that it could become a bad debt.

Service Charge

Mention has been made of the service charge element. Employers view this in different ways and it is a question of which way is regarded as preferable or the most expedient. As a service charge in lieu of gratuities, it is of course right and proper that it should be distributed to the staff for whom it is intended. In some cases it is shared out at the time of receiving it on the basis of an agreed formula. In other cases, sometimes in a seasonal establishment, it is allowed to accumulate and is paid out in one lump sum at the end of the season. The supposed reason for this is to keep some hold on staff who might otherwise walk out on Bank Holiday Monday! This however is all rather by the way and what we are really concerned with is the accountability of it. From an Inland Revenue standpoint the service charge is a remuneration paid to employees. It should, therefore, be added to regular wages paid and P.A.Y.E. calculated and deducted in the usual way. Since service is subject to V.A.T. the total amount of the clients account will be taken through the cash book and other ledgers. When assessing profitability, however, the service charge element should be extracted since, as with V.A.T., the business is merely the custodian of it. Value Added Tax should be deducted from the service charge before distribution to staff.

Trial Balance

To prove the arithmetical accuracy and correct transference of the figures which have been entered through the various ledgers throughout the month, a trial balance should be effected.

Firstly prepare a bank reconciliation statement. This should prove the bank statement as well as the cash book entries. It, therefore, serves a useful double purpose. The next stage is to balance the cash book and the non-bought ledger analysis book together. This is effected by adding the totals of both the bank non-bought ledger and cash non-bought ledger columns together and subtracting the contra entries. The contra entries will be the banking and obtained from the left-hand page of the cash book. To this sub-total should be added the opening balance in the bank column, i.e. the balance of cash at bank brought forward at the start of the financial year. A further sub-total is then struck and from this should be deducted the total balance of non-bought ledger creditors from the previous year, if any. The resultant final set of figures should then agree with the total of the non-bought ledger analysis book.

Balancing Cash Book / Bought Ledger Analysis /
Bought Ledger Account

Each account in the bought ledger should be totalled off to the end of the month. Then carry a running total of all invoices and credits by extracting these from the ledger. The total of unpaid creditors from the previous financial year, i.e. the balances brought forward, should be deducted since these figures have not been entered in the bought ledger analysis book. The resulting sub-total should then tally with the analysis book.

To balance the cash book with the other two ledgers the following procedure should be adopted. Take the end total of the bought ledger bank column in the right-hand side of the cash book. Deduct the balance of the previous year's bought ledger creditors. Add all outstanding invoices. This is effected by carrying a running total of all cheques paid to each creditor in the bought ledger account and subtracting this figure from the running total of invoices less credits which were extracted from the ledger account (see previous paragraph). The figures then obtained should then agree with the other two ledgers.

Balancing Cash Book and Takings Book

It only remains to prove the accuracy of the takings book. To the total of the takings should be added any sundry debtors from the previous financial year and those who have paid in the current year (they will not form part of the current year's takings). To this should be added the opening balance of cash in hand (left-hand cash column) and any receipts shown in the cash book from other sources such as say, H.C.I.T.B. grants, etc. The final total arrived at should agree with the revenue cash column to date. Any difference would indicate either casting errors or omissions in transferring figures from the cash book to the takings book.

The foregoing sounds formidable perhaps in terms of work and time-consuming effort and indeed, possibly insurmountable from the viewpoint of a self-employed practical caterer. This, of course, is probably true. Yet it is quite essential to maintain book work and records if the small caterer is to be successful and know which way he is heading. There are simpler systems as we have said, but the one described in the foregoing pages has suited my own needs for very many years. It is perhaps slightly unorthodox but it does factually provide all the information needed.

Value Added Tax

The introduction of Value Added Tax in 1973 added considerably to the burdens of book-keeping and again it is something which has to be treated with great care. The principles of V.A.T. are by now generally understood and much of the original 'trauma' gone. However, this chapter will not be complete without reference to it and the treatment of 'outputs' and 'inputs'. Fortunately we do not at this time have the problem of different rates of tax in our industry but it could happen. In simple terms, once any item of food or drink, or both, is served to a customer on the premises at a table or counter and service is, therefore, introduced, that item of food or drink is subject to V.A.T. which must be added at the prevailing standard rate. Take-away food is not, at the time of writing, affected. There is some complication when a business is operated which covers both aspects and one part of the takings is subject to V.A.T. and the other not. The two sets of takings figures must be kept separate and distinct in order to satisfy H.M. Customs and Excise, together with some form of identification of sales.

If setting up in business for the first time it would be advisable to consult Customs and Excise with regard to registration as no previous trading figures would be available. At the present time businesses with an annual turnover of less than £15,000 do not have to be registered. It must be remembered, however, that this represents a takings figure of only £288 per week and, more pertinently, if a business is not registered then 'inputs' cannot be reclaimed on items such as ice cream, minerals, fruit juices, liquor, cigarettes and tobacco, cleaning materials and so forth.

Inputs and Outputs

When goods are received on which V.A.T. has been added by the wholesaler or manufacturer, this is known as an 'input tax'. This will apply to items such as those mentioned in the previous paragraph. (Raw foodstuffs are exempted from tax at this time.) Such input tax is reclaimable against output tax on the sales of the business at the end of the quarterly period. It can, therefore, be seen that unless the business is to lose the taxes paid out, a careful record of inputs must be kept.

Accountability of Value Added Tax

H.M. Customs and Excise are in no way concerned if inputs are not reclaimed. They are only interested in the output tax being paid on the sales revenue of the business. If, on the other hand inputs are reclaimed then they will require factual evidence. Any bill or invoice therefore will have to bear the V.A.T. registration number of the vendor from whom you bought the goods, the rate of tax, the address of the vendor and purchaser and the item purchased. If over £50 then it is required that the amount of the tax must be separately shown.

The goods can, of course, be purchases by cash or cheque, from firms for whom the business does not operate a ledger account. In which case they will be non-bought ledger items and will go through the cash book and non-bought ledger analysis book. It is, therefore, necessary to provide a column in the cash book in which to record the amount of V.A.T., but the full amount of the purchase is recorded in the cash or bank column as appropriate. A column is likewise provided in the non-bought ledger analysis. When the amount of the bill or invoice is entered in the analysis book the goods are entered in the appropriate column and the tax in the V.A.T. column. The total amount goes in the end column. At the end of the quarter the amount of non-bought ledger inputs are totalled. Since they are part of the monthly trial balance their arithmetical accuracy will have been proved as long as you have been careful to extract and enter the tax amounts throughout. Since all bills and invoices are given a number it should be easy to identify them should Customs and Excise wish to inspect them.

Similar action is taken with all bought ledger account invoices. When these are received from the supplier the V.A.T. amount is noted and entered in the analysis book only. Since the ledger account is only concerned with the amount of indebtedness to the supplier it is not really necessary to record V.A.T. amounts. At the end of the quarterly period the total of inputs are added to those in the non-bought ledger analysis book and the whole is then reclaimed.

Quarterly Return – Outputs

A return has to be made to Customs and Excise on a form which is sent to every registered trader during the month preceding the end of the quarter. The amount of turnover is declared and the prevailing standard rate of tax is paid on the taxable portion plus any underpayments, if any, for the preceding quarter. As has been noted, the amount of inputs is deducted, as are refunds of overpayment, if applicable.

Inspection

Periodically officers of H.M. Customs and Excise will call to carry out an investigation into the conduct of the business as far as it affects the operation of V.A.T. Needless to say they will need to be satisfied that records are being honestly and satisfactorily maintained. They will require bona fide evidence that the takings figures shown in the books are genuine and that inputs claimed are backed up by the necessary vouchers. There is, and must be, a considerable element of trust but the Department is well aware of the loopholes and is gathering expertise to combat evasion. They do possess considerable powers, as with the Inland Revenue, and it is always wise to keep a clean sheet. The kind of evidence that is needed to support sales revenue are end-totals from till-rolls suitably dated and retained, and copies of all bills which have been issued to a client who has specifically requested a V.A.T. certified invoice are also required. In such cases, if the bill is over £50 the V.A.T. element must be shown separately in the same way as with suppliers.

The foregoing has given some indication, in simple basic terms I hope, of the way V.A.T. affects the business. The best advice that can be given is to go to see Customs and Excise at their local office or, get them to come to see you. They dislike difficulty as much as anyone and will be pleased to help and advise, particularly if you are a newcomer to business.

V.A.T. Deposit Account

It is sensible to keep V.A.T. separate from the business revenue. The best way to handle it is to open a deposit account, or any other similar form of savings account, such as a building society, and let it earn interest. Having calculated what is due to Customs and Excise at the end of each trading week, it can then be paid in. In this way the tax is earning its keep for three months and gives a more realistic picture when looking at the true earnings of the business and the bank balance.

Stores Records

With the keeping of the main books of account and other back-up statistical records, it is necessary to record receipts and issues of all goods. The ability to evaluate stocks as assets has been mentioned earlier in this chapter. The subject of stock control is enlarged on in Chapter 9.

The Safe

Security of cash is important and the insurers will naturally be interested in the form that such safeguards take. A good strong safe is a wise investment. It should be of reputable manufacture and should either be securely fitted into the wall, bolted through to the floor joists or fixed to concrete. A safe which is not so secured can be transported and opened at a more convenient place! The insurers will also wish to know the extent of cash normally carried on the premises and the frequency of banking as well as the amount in transit. It is usual for a duplicate key to be kept at the bank under seal.

CHAPTER 7

Costing and Profitability

Brief reference was made in Chapter 6 to 'working percentages' in the context of record and statistics keeping. The ultimate objective of any business enterprise must be to achieve a satisfactory trading profit. This can only be effected by sound costing and by setting percentage targets of profitability and meeting them.

Effect of Trading Policy

When an existing business has been taken over, the trading policy will have been predecided to a large extent, unless changed. However, opening a new enterprise will call for a particular marketing strategy and policy. As we have seen in earlier chapters this will be the result of a feasibility study based on consumer need. The chosen style of operation, and the consequent level of overheads associated with it will effectively determine the price structure and basis of the costings. To illustrate the point, a simple café business will not offer the same standards of comfort and appointments as a high-class restaurant. Its staffing needs will be simpler and staff need not be so technicaly skilled, or as highly paid. Equipment will probably not require to be so comprehensive; laundry costs and fuel bills will be lower. The costs of renewals and replacements of furnishings will again only be fractional.

Initial capital costs will be lower and the need to see a higher return will not be so evident. Rent and rates need not necessarily be very different, however, in similar-sized premises, but certainly all other overheads will be.

Accepting this fact, a much higher gross profit will have to be earned in the restaurant as against that for the café in order to cover such higher overheads and yield a satisfactory net profit finally. Let us try to show, without I hope oversimplifying, the difference between gross and net profit. The difference between the cost price in raw materials and the selling price of the completed dish is gross profit. What then remains after taking into account all the operational costs of the business is net profit, before taxation.

This simple illustration may help to understand the kind of breakdown: cost of raw materials 40p; selling price 100p. The gross profit in this instance would be 60p. There is a 40 per cent food cost and a 60 per cent gross profit. If we say that the cost of overheads represented 40p, this would then leave 20p on the dish as net profit before tax. Unfortunately, in practice it is not quite as simple as that, but it serves to illustrate the point.

Food Cost

By 'food cost' we mean the actual cost to the caterer of the raw materials in a dish or beverage, etc. We are not concerned with the cost of preparing it, which is principally wages and fuel. If a joint of meat cost £10.00 and it yielded twenty portions, the cost per portion would be 50p. It would have to have a mark-up price on the menu of £1.25 to produce a 60 per cent gross profit. To put it another way it would be necessary to apply a $33\frac{1}{3}$ per cent food cost which in effect means charging three times the cost price; alternatively, a 50 per cent food cost would be twice the cost.

Costing Yield

Costing out single items is quite easy. An 8 oz. rump steak costs £1.50. If the policy is to work on a $33\frac{1}{3}$ per cent food cost then the selling price would be £4.50; a 40 per cent cost gives £3.75, and a 50 per cent cost £3.00. Where, however, it is necessary to calculate yield from a batch, cuts from a joint, or even portions from a bag of potatoes, more experience then becomes necessary. Regard must be taken of losses in cooking or wastage in preparation for example. If it is expected to get say twenty 4 oz. portions of meat from a 5 lb joint one might find a 20 per cent cooking loss which would bring the yield down to only sixteen in practice. Were the selling price fixed on the expected yield of twenty portions it would obviously be insufficient to realise the proper gross profit. Losses in bone weight must also be allowed for, as well as trimming of fat.

Again, it is necessary to know how many peach halves there are in a tin, or how many portions of solid pack apples a tin will yield. Without this research and knowledge costing becomes a 'hit and miss' affair and pure 'guesstimation'.

The experienced caterer probably knows within quite fine limits what he can expect. He can look at a turkey perhaps and instinctively know that a 20 lb oven-ready bird will produce thirty portions or that an A10 size of solid pack fruit will fill a certain-sized baking dish and produce X number of portions of pie. It is still 'hit or miss' but less risky because he has done it for years. To the newcomer however, not being armed with that kind of knowledge, the only safe way is to work to recipes, particularly where 'made-up' dishes are concerned.

Working to Recipes

By this we do not necessarily mean the cookery page from your favourite magazine! There is nothing to stop the budding caterer from using recipes from any source, however, as long as they are properly costed. Once this is done they can be filed and used as a constant reference and guide. Developing one's own library based on dishes as they are introduced into the table d'hôte menu is a good idea. Agreed, it is a bit more paperwork and tedium but there are many advantages and some of our major companies have seen fit to introduce such a system into their operations. The introduction of recipes gives constant quality control and when new kitchen staff start employment they have ready-made guidelines to work to.

The recipe should contain not only all the listed ingredients but their weights and, above all, their cost. The yield in portions is then identified and then the cost per unit, which is a permanent record to which to refer. Updating of prices is, of course, essential or, as a costing tool, it becomes useless. By taking the unit portion cost price and multiplying it by the percentage factor we arrive at the selling price. For example the unit cost price may be 25p. If the house policy is to work on 33⅓ per cent then it will sell at 75p.

If the recipe is to be used to assist kitchen staff, which is not a costing factor but an organisational one, then the method of preparation would be written in also.

It is a fact that whilst the policy may be to decide on a particular food percentage it does not necessarily follow that all dishes will be rigidly so costed. The aim should be to achieve the desired percentage overall. It is often the case that certain dishes can earn considerably more and others less. In the instance of a permanently printed menu one may find that seasonal fluctuations in prices of raw materials may cause a 'swings and roundabouts' situation. In another case the caterer may decide that if he were to charge the proper price as dictated by the norm, he would not sell that particular dish. One argument might be to drop it from the menu immediately but he may decide to keep it for prestige purposes and be content with it earning less. The important principle is to see that the overall percentage is maintained.

The Gross Profit

Why a 33⅓, 40 or 50 per cent food costing? How does it affect final net profitability – which is why you are in business? Quite simply, the greater the level of overheads then the more the caterer must charge to cover them. This comes back to the trading policy. When setting up there will be certain financial commitments which will be known. Rent and rates are a prime example. It should also be possible within reason to estimate wages and National Health Insurance. Fuel, light and power is something of a variable, for whilst lighting and heating has to be there whether the restaurant is empty or full, there is always a tendency to use more if kitchen equipment is in constant and heavy use when busy of course. This, however, is fortunately well taken care of in the additional revenue the extra business accrues. Laundry charges too will increase with the additional trade. As the level of business increases the ratio of fixed overheads declines. There are, of course, a large variety of overheads which vary from business to business. One may hire some items of equipment, another may advertise heavily, and so on. The spread of capitalisation, redecoration and repairs to property, maintenance of plant, insurance, office expenses, etc., are all factors which affect profitability, so all of these things will affect the price structure of the menu. The level of prices to be charged must then be carefully considered in the light of all known or, at least, realistically assessed operating costs. This is not easy to do when opening a new venture and yet it is essential to quantify such costs if a satisfactory level of profitability is to be attained.

Let us say that in a small café the assessed overheads were £150 per week, and it is wise to err on the heavy side allowing for all contingencies. It has been decided, because of the style of business to operate competitively on a 50 per cent food cost; then, takings of £500 per week would mean an expected pre-tax net profit of £100. This can be illustrated as follows.

Takings		£500	
Food costs	£250		(50% Gross profit)
Operating costs	£150		
Total costs		£400	
Net profit		£100	(20% Net profit)

The breakeven point would be takings of £300 per week before profits were being earned. It is important to know this.

This example is very simple and is not representative of balance sheet format where, for example, depreciation would be offset against net profit. It does however show how to structure costings in the light of profitability, and how the level of selling prices must be decided. The examples above are only intended to show the mechanics, and are not necessarily representative.

Inflation

In a period of inflation, overheads in the form of wages, fuel, light and power, office expenses, rates, sometimes rise quite steeply. It is therefore pertinent that these should be constantly reviewed in relation to one's selling prices even though the basic cost of raw materials may remain stable. This is where record-keeping starts to tell its story.

Controlling Wastage

It is pointless to carry out a careful exercise in costing if a wary eye is not kept at all times on wastages. This can be wastage of raw materials caused through over-buying, bad utilisation, poor storage, wasteful cutting in preparation, over-preparation through misjudging business, and other such things.

Other forms of waste are caused through gas rings or electric equipment being left switched on when not needed, heating and lighting being unnecessarily used, staff not being gainfully occupied or having too many on duty at known slacker periods, thus creating a high wage cost factor. Wages often account for the largest share of operating costs. However, a great deal depends on the style of business, as we have seen.

Staff Meals

Staff ordinarily receive meals on duty as part of their wage structure. It is wise to lay down hard and fast rules as to what they may or may not have or misunderstanding occurs. The regulations specify a meal of sufficient quality and quantity. Whilst it obviously depends on the number of staff employed, it is worth preparing a special staff meal and for it to be eaten at a specified period. The meal should be costed out and kept within the bounds of reason. If such an approach is not used then the caterer will find that his staff are eating better than he can afford to. This danger is inherent in the practice of waiting to see what is left from lunch before deciding what to give them. There may be nothing and the handiest thing is a fillet steak – which is not conducive to good profits. If it is left to the chef to produce his kitchen percentage then the cost of staff meals should be credited to him.

Utilisation

The skilful utilisation of 'left-overs' is something of an art and indeed a book could well be written on the subject. One must, of course, be careful not to throw good money after bad and it is very important never to take risks in reheating or reprocessing any food which is likely to be a hazard to health. However, profits can be preserved by good kitchen economy and within the limits of good sense and culinary skill. Food should never be thrown away should there be a good chance of it earning money. Utilisation is one of the problems of the table d'hôte menu. An à la carte menu does not have such drawbacks, since the meals are cooked to order.

Simplicity

There is much to commend the simple menu approach. Simplicity means that the waste risk is reduced and that the operation is more controllable. By concentrating effort on the fewer items there are benefits such as lower wage costs which immediately contribute to higher profitability, and in the fast food style of business mean faster turnover of seating too.

Control and Accounts

The beneficial effects of a good control system have already been discussed. Profitability and control go hand in hand. Without the means of charting progress and preventing losses through one way or another, it is virtually impossible to check. The trading policy is defined, the level of prices and percentages to be earned are established, but without the machinery to prove effectiveness it is all a wasted exercise.

A target is something to aim at. Targets of profitability are just that.

CHAPTER 8

Purchasing

Importance of Quality

One of the key factors in good profitability is a sound purchasing policy. Probably the first thing one thinks of in this
connection is to buy as cheaply as possible. Buying competitively and buying cheaply are two different matters. Goods
which are cheap are usually substandard in quality and, in the
end mean wastage, poor economy and often customer dis-
satisfaction. If the restaurant is trying to achieve a high
reputation, which should always be the objective, then quality
should never be sacrificed.

In this context, quality should not necessarily be confused
with expensive goods. In the lowest price trade bracket, with a
'beans on toast' type of offering, it is, if you like, possible to
buy poor quality baked beans in a rather colourless and taste-
less sauce. Naturally there is the temptation to buy as cheaply
as possible because of the, probably, very competitive price
structure of the menu. Yet, paying a bit more and charging
comensurately for a better quality item could well contribute
to a better reputation and building of sales.

To go to the other end of the scale, if you purchase frozen
beef fillets which, as well as being frozen, are also cheaper
because they are small, perhaps only weighing at most $3\frac{1}{2}$lb,
they will invariably be of poor eating quality and there will be

difficulty to cut a fillet steak of sufficient size, together with considerable 'tail' wastage. True, it is possible to use 'tail fillet' for many items such as 'Bitoks' or 'Strogonoff', etc., but if the prime purpose of buying fillets was to satisfy a demand for fillet steaks (or for Chateaubriand) then the purchasing was badly misguided. Far better to have bought 5/6 lb 'Cryovac' or fresh fillets in the first place, paid more for them and charged accordingly.

The same goes for fish and vegetables, frozen foods, or whatever. If the yield from a cheaper item, or brand of tinned goods, is going to prove less, and the overall quality poor and unsatisfactory, then there has been little point in the exercise. Shop around and buy competively by all means, for this is what good sensible buying is all about; but purchasing 'on the cheap' is often a misguided policy, it invariably means wastage in the kitchen and even a discontented chef or cook, as well as a dissatisfied client.

Sources of Supply

The usual sources of supply are from a wholesaler, direct from the manufacturer, from a 'cash and carry' outlet or from the markets. The purchasing policy will usually be influenced by the size and scope of the business. However, the average business will, in practice, often take full advantage of a combination of sources. Putting complete reliance on a single supply source usually means a restriction on choice and the inability to purchase competitively. Those who are tied to a franchise agreement, however, will in any case be restricted to a certain extent, depending on their contract.

Cash and carry

The growth in recent years of the cash and carry outlet has probably influenced the buying habits of smaller caterers more than any other factor. Many of them were started by wholesale suppliers to the grocery and catering trades, using their warehouses for the base of the operation. The growth has been rapid and now one sees diversification with meat, vegetables and frozen food departments operating in purpose-built warehouses all over the country, particularly on trading estates which are yet another manifestation of modern merchandising and planning. Supermarkets, however, can offer competition.

Most of the companies that operate cash and carry outlets still maintain a delivery service. Since the supplier, however, has to bear the costs of transport overheads as well as credit, possibly over a monthly period, prices will be higher on goods so delivered. Many also insist on a minimum-value order to make the delivery economical for them. The philosophy, therefore, is to try to get the caterer to collect his own stores and let him bear such costs in exchange for a more competitive price.

Cash and carry warehouses can vary in their offerings, some having a bias towards catering and others towards the smaller shopkeeper. It is, therefore, worth shopping around if you are fortunate to have a choice in the area. Prices often vary fractionally but there is not, in my experience certainly, sufficient difference overall to warrant the time and expense of driving around from one to another to save the odd 'coppers'. The necessity is more likely to arise because one warehouse is out of stock of specific items that are urgently needed.

There are both advantages and disadvantages of using the cash and carry system. One must of course run a vehicle – a van or a heavy duty estate car being the most adaptable. It must be insured to carry goods in connection with one's business. If it is taxed as a 'Goods Vehicle' it has to be weighed and a higher rate of road fund licence paid. There are advantages in so taxing however, particularly from an Inland Revenue standpoint, which make studying this angle worthwhile. Visiting cash and carry can be time consuming according to the distance and the efficiency of the checkouts operated. In a small, virtually single-handed business this can be difficult unless you close in the afternoon, when you should probably be resting. On the other hand, of course, the advantages are cheaper prices (but do not forget to offset your own time, the vehicle running costs and having to pay cash), being able to pick and choose what you buy and in smaller quantities, the opportunity to compare prices and quality, etc. A further benefit is being able to pick up goods quickly if you find yourself in need through some circumstance.

One last point. It is necessary to apply for a 'card' since 'cash and carry' only operates for bona fide traders. A letter-head or other identity is all that is necessary usually although references are required, of course, should you envisage paying by cheque at any time. In which case a limit is often applied.

Fish

Fish can be bought direct from any of the fish ports and from any of the London-based wholesalers who will supply weekly lists of prices. A telephone call with the order will usually mean an early morning delivery next day. Alternatively it may be preferable to buy locally with a special discount arrangement. This has the advantage of being able to buy in smaller quantities as you need them should the demand not warrant the former arrangement. Many small caterers depend on their deep-freeze cabinet, or as we have seen, on cash and carry. Frozen fish apart, it should always be the policy to buy as freshly as possible, choosing fish with firm flesh, bright eyes and free from smell. Correct storage thereafter is important. If such refrigerated storage is a difficulty then it should be the policy to buy only sufficient for the envisaged day's trade. Better for the fish to be 'off' in one sense than the other!

Meat

The meat-buying policy will almost certainly depend on various factors, the type of menu and the size of the business being the two most likely to affect considerations. Buying whole lambs or quarters of beef direct from the market, or even ex-farm, is only feasible if the trade is very substantial, the menu can absorb all the various cuts and, above all, there is a larger chef or butcher who is capable of processing the carcases economically. In the ordinary way it is not to be recommended. Considerable cold-room facilities are needed too.

Apart from some companies specialising in sales to caterers, some of the provincial wholesalers will only supply butcher's shops. The best arrangement for the smaller caterer is to negotiate special prices with a local butcher and either to supply items at an agreed cut, weight and size (e.g. 6 or 8 oz.

rump steaks) or to supply whole sirloins, rumps or say, best ends of lamb, etc., and then butcher oneself. There are advantages with the latter. For example, one can purchase a whole sirloin and after taking off the flank for use in puddings and pies, there is a good fillet for steaks and the loin for entrecôtes, bones for the stock pot and some fat for rendering down for frying, etc. This is good economy.

The importance of quality has been stressed at the commencement of this chapter. It is probably more important in the field of meat buying than any other. Few items cause more trouble or invite criticism at the table than tough meat, particularly steaks. The old conception of recognising quality was to select beef that had creamy white fat and a bright cherry red flesh which was firm to the touch and with a nice grain. This is still true but so much cross-breeding has taken place in recent years that this old yardstick is not always a fair test. The flesh of some Highland cattle can be quite dark but still eat very well. The fat of some cattle primarily bred for dairy farming is often a bright yellow. The experienced buyer can recognise by the grain and general appearance and firmness of touch, but for the less experienced the best guarantee is to pin one's faith on the reputation of the butcher.

Poultry and Game

There is an abundance of frozen chickens and ducklings, etc., normally available through the usual outlets. Whilst these have to be resorted to on occasions, there is much to be said for buying the fresh article in preference. Defrosting process often accounts for a loss in weight and birds tend to cook drier and with less flavour. If, therefore, a connection can be made with a farm it is worth it since there is very often little difference in price and on occasions there could well be a price advantage. Otherwise fresh birds are, of course, available from wholesalers or butchers. The same applies to turkeys.

When talking prices, however, remember to check whether birds are 'rough plucked' or 'oven-ready'. Rough plucked can sometimes mean that there is a fair bit of work still to be done. 'Clean plucked' does mean that all feathers should have been removed, but in either case the birds will be complete with entrails and will have to be drawn and, in the case of turkeys, the leg sinews will have to be pulled. All this means a lot of work in the kitchen which is, of course, the reason for the swing over to the frozen oven-ready article by the trade. Fresh birds can be supplied oven-ready however. For supplies of game such as pheasant, partridge and grouse, hares, etc., it is best to approach a firm specialising in this field, although a connection can sometimes be established with a 'shoot'.

Frozen Foods

The tremendous growth of the frozen-food industry has meant considerable competition within it and a very wide range of offerings both in brands and in types of food. One of the earlier problems in the industry was a complete lack of agreement over the problem of size grading. This is being overcome but since a large proportion of frozen foods come from all over the world there are still difficulties. Quality varies considerably and it is really a question of combing the market to gain knowledge of what suits best. Two differing brands of, say, broccoli or asparagus spears can be totally different in appearance. Company 'A's' 'Standard Quality' peas can be a very different proposition to Company 'B's' and so on. The same applies particularly to scampis. Availability too tends to be erratic sometimes. It is not, therefore, a good idea to be tied to one particular supplier. One blessing, more often than not, is that one can usually see what one is buying since, unlike tinned goods, the product is at least in a transparent pack!

Canned Foods

One cannot unfortunately see inside a can, unlike polythene packs, without opening it. Once again there can be a great variation in quality and in what we call 'drained weight'. In effect this means the actual weight of the contents once liquor has been drained off. The 'count' too in the case of say, peach or pear halves is important. In the case of apples or black-currants, etc., it is better to buy what is known as 'solid pack'.

Generally I have always found that you get what you pay for. Quite often one is offered a brand that has never been heard of before and at a very cheap price. Rarely however does it ever prove much of a bargain. The products of well-known reputable canning firms are usually the safest bet. However, it is a question of experience for what one company produces very well another seems to fail on and vice versa. Do not be afraid to carry out tests, not only of flavour and appearance, but more particularly of drained weight – the price per dry pound will sometimes give the unwary caterer quite a surprise.

Dry Goods

With the more specialised items like tea and coffee, particularly the latter, it usually pays to go to a merchant. Water varies in hardness quite a lot from area to area and an experienced tea and coffee merchant will be able to advise and help choose what is best. The kind of blend and roast can also be carefully chosen to suit the particular type of trade that one is doing as well as deciding the unit weight of package to suit brewing apparatus, e.g. $3\frac{1}{2}$ or 4 oz. packs for 'Cona' equipment.

Goods such as sugar or flour can be obtained in cwt or sacks. There is obviously an advantage price-wise in buying such quantities but for the small caterer it might prove handier and more economical to buy in smaller units – particularly if dealing largely with cash and carry. You have to hump it!

Vegetables and Fruit

Due largely to the increasing difficulty in obtaining staff to prepare them, the trade has turned away from fresh vegetables, which is regrettable, for a reputation awaits the restaurateur who specialises in them. Here the purchasing policy rather depends on the locality of the business and whether it is near one of the markets or in a country area. In other cases it means a delivery from a local wholesaler or a trip to the cash and carry should they have a vegetable department. Whatever the supply source, however, vegetables or salad stuffs should always be bought as freshly as possible and the produce examined carefully. Imported items are usually well packaged and cases should therefore never be accepted without sample checking. This particularly applies to tomatoes, lemons and other citrus fruits, avocados, melons, etc. Condition is important and since many items come from abroad, they may be unripe or 'backward' or, of course, overripe. A few 'wet' tomatoes can quickly cause the rest in a 'boat' to go bad. The avocados may be hard and unfit to serve for several days and the same applies to melons of the various types. Sprouts and peas heat up in their bags and can go bad very quickly. Buy only sufficient, therefore, for immediate needs. Be particularly careful of vegetables, lettuce, etc., which have been packed in a wet condition. If they are to be used immediately there is no problem but otherwise there will be difficulties in keeping.

Ensure that you buy the correct type of potato for your needs. 'King Edward' or red potatoes are best for boiling; 'Majestics' or whites for chipping and frying generally. When buying cauliflowers choose if possible the smaller type with nice tight 'flowers' as they will cook better and cut up easier for portioning, the large loose kind tending to break up leading to wastage. The same applies to Brussels sprouts, the 'blown' type tending to cook 'mushy'.

Root vegetables are not usually much of a problem but new season's carrots and turnips do not store as well as their elders.

The purchasing of fruit is, I feel, reasonably straightforward except perhaps for the already stressed words of caution regarding examination for condition and ripeness. If, of course, the fruit is for immediate use in fruit salad it is sometimes possible to buy a few bargains that are a bit 'wastey'. For the fruit basket in the restaurant, however, only fruit of the finest quality should be bought since it is something of a show-piece. In this connection it is often wisest to buy in small quantities from a local fruiterer of good repute.

Paperware

Paper serviettes, kitchen towels, doylies, dish papers, greaseproof, toilet rolls and other disposables together often form quite a surprising part of a caterer's overheads these days. Many of the manufacturers will supply direct with quantity discounts if sufficient bulk is ordered. Cash and carry outlets stock all the items usually, which allow smaller quantities to be purchased. Serviettes are obtainable in various sizes and finishes. For the better class trade a larger, three-ply article is best which is usually available in a range of colours, while for the popular class trade a smaller single ply is usually acceptable. Prices can vary, so it is therefore worth shopping around; but if storage does not pose too great a problem, then the direct manufacturer contact is the most advantageous.

Detergents and Cleaning Materials

Always buy in commercial sizes and quantities and direct from manufacturers if possible. This will effect a considerable price saving, particularly in liquid detergents, soda and soap powders.

Cash and carry outlets usually carry stocks of wire wool, floor cloths, dish cloths as well as brooms, brushes and other items needed for cleaning.

CHAPTER 9

Stores and Store-keeping

Stores are assets. As such they have to be paid for and they represent the raw materials on which profit will be earned. If such materials are not stored correctly so that wastage occurs, or securely so that they may be pilfered, serious inroads into profitability will occur.

Storerooms

In small business premises space is usually at a premium and, when the premises have been adapted from some other original purpose, often not ideal. Finding space, therefore, which offers correct storage conditions is not always easy. In the perfect situation, three or four separate categories of storage facilities should exist. Dry goods, greengrocery, liquor and tobacco, also cold-room and deep-freeze facilities. As business grows so does the demand on storage space and refrigeration; the problem becomes increasingly acute and most small businesses suffer in this direction. In the less frequent event of planning new premises, however, it is possible to give proper consideration to storage needs.

Dry Stores

Good ventilation should be provided to allow free circulation of air thus avoiding condensation and mustiness. Shelving should be arranged in bays after taking into careful consideration the known sizes of cases of say, A10 size tins or other sizes which are most likely to be used. If this is done first and then measurements between shelves and supports arranged accordingly, considerable space saving will be achieved. Galvanised metal bins should be used to store any goods which are likely to be attacked by vermin. The store should be as spacious as possible and be well lit and dry. Any dampness will soon affect the quality of flour, sugar, tea and coffee, salt or such goods which absorb moisture. All goods should, in any case, be kept free of the floor, pallets being the best thing to use. These can be taken out from time to time, scrubbed and thoroughly dried. It is important to keep the store clean and swept out regularly. The Food and Drugs (Control of Food Premises) Act 1976 empowers the local Environmental Health Officer to apply to the Court for an 'emergency closure' of any premises within three days if he considers that there is an imminent risk of danger to health. While not so concerned with cleanliness as such, any goods which can affect each other by their strong or characteristic smell, such as soap or detergents, should always be stored away from foodstuffs. Try and keep a separate store for cleaning materials.

The store should be arranged so that stocktaking is made easy, and goods arranged in a systematic way so as to facilitate proper rotation and turnover of stock. Whilst in existing premises some compromise may have to be made, the ideal situation for the main dry stores would be adjacent to the kitchen and, of course, on ground floor level. If all stocks have to be carried or lifted up to a first or second floor it will make for heavy work. If, therefore, the situation allows for a rear delivery entrance with both stores and kitchen adjacent, this would constitute the best arrangement.

Vegetable Store

Greengrocery, saladstuffs, potatoes, etc., require a different storage approach and can be effectively combined with a vegetable preparation area, again adjacent to the kitchen to be workable. Here a cool temperature is essential to preserve the storage of perishables, such as lettuce and green vegetables generally, as much as possible. The floor should be quarry tiled so that it can be kept clean, particularly if the store is used for preparation. In which case white ceramic-tiled walls too will be conducive to keeping the temperature cool and promoting good hygiene practice. Sinks and plenty of cold running water, potato peeling and possibly chipping equipment, plus galvanised work tables will complete the vegetable and salad preparation part. A drainage galley let into the floor is wise since there is usually water spillage, although if the potato peeling equipment is set in a corner with a kerbing round, and with its own drainage, this will help to minimise a wet floor condition. The work surfaces should be well lit, but too much light should be kept away from green vegetables and saladstuffs stored there if this is at all possible. The workers should be able to stand on wooden pallets to keep their feet dry.

All goods should be kept clear of the floor on wooden pallets to prevent sacks from getting damp and to assist cleaning. Shelving should be arranged, again taking box measurements into account to permit maximum utilisation of space.

Daily inspection of all perishables is important to ensure that odd bad items do not start a trend. Proper rotation of stocks is, therefore, essential. Staff have a habit of taking the best items first instead of those which perhaps require trimming.

Liquor Store

Security is paramount where liquor and tobacco are concerned. Whilst we shall deal with the record aspect shortly, by security we mean safe and pilfer-proof. Strong doors, security bars at windows, and above all an expensive lever-type lock and not a rim-latch which can be opened with a plastic scraper! Even an average restaurant can be obliged to keep a large amount of stock on occasions, such as in the 'festive season'. As long as there is reasonable ventilation such as that provided by air bricks, it is probably better not to have windows, a cellar being ideal in this respect both in temperature as well as security.

The store should be racked from floor to ceiling with some shelving for spirits and liqueurs, with others forming 'bins' for wines which should all be clearly numbered conforming to the wine list. This facilitates stocktaking. Whilst it does not matter if spirits, fortified wines and liqueurs, etc., are stored upright, it is essential for all wines to be laid on their side and, in the case of rarer examples and slow movers, occasionally carefully turned.

Beer Store

Beers are often kept separately stored. They are not, of course, as valuable and, whilst they should be kept safely, are not so attractive to a thief. No one is so likely to steal a ten-gallon keg as say a bottle of brandy. The liquor store could be on a first floor but beer storage, owing to the weight of such items, is better at ground level depending on the situation of the bars. In so far as restaurants are concerned, keg beer or lager is most likely to be of interest and reference to barrels, etc., is not really applicable. The publican's art is a somewhat different one.

Records and Stock Control

To safeguard assets such as stocks, to assess consumption satisfactorily and to know the stock position, further record-keeping is essential. Apart from other considerations it is necessary to be able to evaluate stocks periodically as we have seen in Chapter 6, to ascertain the true financial position of the business at any time and to calculate gross profit.

Stock Books

It is easy to obtain purpose-designed books. There should be columns ruled for each class of goods, date, price paid and quantities. It is not necessary to overcomplicate and whatever system is the most practical and effective can be used. The essentials are to know what goods are in stock, how much they cost and when received, what has been issued, to whom, and the stock level to be maintained. The caterer can go about this in many ways and a lot of complication can be introduced, but he is a busy chap and as long as those essential facts mentioned above are recognised and recorded, it is all that really matters. It is, however, worth going into a little more detail to underline the practicalities.

Ordering

Always try to place orders in writing. This obviates subsequent argument when a delivery is wrong and in addition, acts as an *aide-mémoire* and a record. A telephoned order, if taking a long time before delivery by the supplier, is often difficult to recall and in many cases it is as well to put a confirmation in the post. On occasions the supplier insists on this procedure in any case to protect himself. A carbon-copy type book is best for this and should number consecutively. A dated record of orders is thus in existence.

Goods Received

When goods are received they should immediately be checked against the invoice or delivery note, without which they should not be accepted. It should be verified that the goods are in fact those which were ordered, that they are in good condition and of the correct quantity. Price should also be checked against quotation but the vendor often protects himself by a price ruling at the time of delivery. If all is satisfactory then the goods can be received into the store and stacked away systematically.

Having received the goods they should be entered in the stock book, added to existing stock level figures and any price increases noted and annotated (see Figure 2).

Goods Issued

Some form of effective control should be exercised by the caterer over issues, and staff not just allowed to help themselves to whatever they think is needed for the day's work. The proprietor, chef or cook, restaurant supervisor, or other responsible head of department, should indent in a book or by some other means for whatever is required for the day's business. If then it is possible to issue the stores for the day at a predecided time, say 9.00 a.m., it will simplify matters considerably and will avoid the stores being opened up every few minutes for some odd small item. It weakens security when this is allowed to happen and particularly so when an item is wanted during peak periods and the member of staff has not time to book it out. It makes nonsense of stock-keeping. The key to any stores should always be kept by the manager or proprietor.

The issue books, or slips, are then taken to the office and the issues deducted from the stock level shown in the stock book for that day and a new balance struck.

Figure 2. Suggested form of stock sheet which can be adapted for whatever purpose required.

		Commodity	
		Salad Cream	Gherkins
Unit Cost Unit Size			
19.2.75	Stock	4	3
	Receipts	2	–
	Issues	3	–
20.2.75	Stock	3	3
	Receipts	–	–
	Issues	1	2
21.2.75	Stock	2	1
	Receipts	–	2
	Issues	–	–
22.2.75	Stock	2	3
	Receipts	–	–
	Issues	–	1
23.2.75	Stock	2	2

Stock Levels

Experience dictates what particular levels should be maintained of any one commodity. The rate of usage, once known and recognised by the volume of issues recorded, decides the safe level to be held. This is a useful guide to anyone required to carry out the ordering function in the absence of the proprietor. If, however, it is known that prices of certain commodities are going to jump, and it is prudent to buy heavily, this is a purchasing decision which would override stock level policy.

Physical Stocktaking

A physical check of the stock should be taken at least weekly. Writing up from daily issue books is all very well but go round and see that what *should* be there is in fact there. It is the only safeguard against pilferage for otherwise a stock deficiency could go unnoticed for weeks and the thief be encouraged to take more. If the stock does not match up, carry out a full inquiry. Do not let it go by the board, or the staff will assume you are not concerned.

Cold Stores

Security is much more difficult in the area of cold-room storage. Whilst smaller cabinets can be stocked for immediate service purposes, it is often necessary to open the cold room in some circumstances such as during heavy business. However, it should be possible to padlock it at night. Control can be effected, of course, as necessary. If forty rump steaks are issued from the cold room for service, and the waiter checks reveal thirty-six have been sold, then four should be returned to storage. However, the cold room, more than likely, will carry everything from milk to mise en place for the hors d'oeuvre trolley, reserves of sweet dishes, and just about everything else that needs to be kept cold. The same goes for the deep-freeze as far as security is concerned. It is not practical to treat it in the same way as the dry or liquor store. We have to trust people sometimes, although caterers live in a suspicious world.

A cold store stock book should be kept as well as a record of frozen-food purchases and issues. The same principles apply and the maintenance of stock levels is just as important.

In whatever form it is decided to keep stock books, as long as they are kept accurately and inform the caterer of all the required facts for the purposes of purchasing and accounting, and for preventing losses, then the work involved will be well rewarded in terms of efficiency. Stock is, in effect, the same as cash and must be regarded in precisely the same way.

CHAPTER 10

The Menu

Policy Approach

'What kind of menu shall we offer?' This is one of the first questions that the caterer just setting up will usually ponder over. It is a policy decision which will probably affect the future of the business more than any other since the whole character of the restaurant will depend on it. Being so critical, it is a decision which must be well considered in the light of many factors. Earlier in the book the need was stressed for a sound feasibility study into local consumer requirement and the kind of trade which will best satisfy it. Assuming this has been done, the next considerations are the ability of the proprietor and his expertise to follow such a policy through, the possibilities of being able to staff the business satisfactorily, and to ensure that the premises are suitably adaptable and equipped.

Types of Menu

There are basically two kinds of menu, à la carte and table d'hôte. Whilst these will be described in greater detail presently, in simple terms à la carte gives total freedom of choice from a menu containing a number of items individually priced, whereas table d'hôte offers a fixed number of courses at a fixed price, albeit possibly with a choice of alternatives.

129

Either of them can, of course, be reduced to comparative simplicity or, conversely, be complicated, complex and elaborate.

Advantages

The à la carte menu, within the context of the above description, covers a very wide field of presentation. This is particularly so in the field of fast food restaurants and speciality houses such as Pizza Parlours, etc., as opposed to the traditional full-scale menu found in the more orthodox restaurant.

The advantages of the à la carte menu are considerable, the principal one being that of possible simplicity. Eliminated is the need for daily menu planning and all that means in terms of costing out and working to recipes, advance planning, requisitioning from a larger number of suppliers with consequent complications of accounting, and daily writing or printing of menus, etc. Gone too is the problem of wastage and of economically dealing with the difficult question of utilising 'left-overs' satisfactorily. Depending on the type of operation and menu, staffing can be easier too, since a simple menu is not so demanding in terms of the need for skilled staff. A further bonus is that the menu can be operated continuously over long hours since food is only cooked when ordered, thus encouraging a maximum revenue turnover per seat. The only occasions that the menu needs reprinting is when repricing takes place or some innovation such as the introduction of a new dish to stimulate interest and sales.

So much for the advantages. The disadvantages are minimal in comparison. Except in a fast food outlet which often depends largely on passing trade, the à la carte menu tends to be inflexible and monotonous to a regular clientele. One way of overcoming this is to introduce a 'Special Dish of the Day' or 'Chef's Special'. This can usefully supplement the standard menu and the dish can be priced competitively to assist in retaining a strong regular trade particularly over the lunch period. Experience is often the best guide and if one finds one's customers regularly asking for a certain dish then it is worth heeding an obvious demand. It does not do though to take too much notice of occasional requests as one cannot supply everything! Once the policy is agreed, unless it is obviously wrong, it should be left to develop.

A la carte Menu

A la carte means literally 'as the card' implying a completely free choice on the part of the diner to arrange his meal according to his whims and fancies and of course his pocket. There is a sequence of courses which tradition and gastronomic sense has followed for centuries, the meal starting with dishes of a light nature serving to excite and stimulate the palate, followed by more substantial courses and finishing with sweets, cheese or savouries. Modern pressures of living and economic considerations often mean nowadays that the average diner requires only three courses or less. The à la carte menu should, therefore, be arranged in various sections in the traditional order and according to the degree of complication or simplicity desired.

It is customary to list in the first section what are rather baldly and unattractively headed 'Starters' in modern terminology. Hors d'Oeuvre, or Appetisers, sounds better. Included are usually the house hors d'oeuvre and items such as smoked salmon, smoked trout, potted shrimps, melon, prawn cocktail, grapefruit, egg mayonnaise, fruit juice, etc.

A second section would be headed Soups and would contain simply perhaps one or two 'Soups of the Day' leaving the waiter/waitress to inform the customer what these are, or a more comprehensive list of the main types. Further sections can then be devoted to egg dishes, omelettes, etc., and perhaps another to pasta such as ravioli, spaghetti, canneloni and so on. There then follows a section headed Fish covering grilled, deep-fried, meunière, poached, etc., with appropriate garnishes or sauces.

Sections for entrées, roasts and grills can be generally placed under one heading of Meats for convenience, or separately if preferred. A selection of vegetables is sometimes included in the price of any main dish. However it is not unusual for vegetables to be separately listed and priced. A further section can be devoted to salads. This can refer to green salads or composite salads, coleslaw, etc., or can embrace cold main dishes such as Chicken, Ham, Egg and Cheese, etc. Alternatively a complete Cold Buffet section might appear listing say Ribs of Beef, Tongue, Salmon, etc.

The menu is completed with further sections for Sweets, Savouries, and Cheeses. Where there is no cover charge in operation it is usual to show a section for sundries, rolls and butter, French bread, etc. Beverages quite often include a range of speciality coffees such as Irish (Gaelic), Calypso, French, etc., and these can be featured strongly as a selling point.

Obviously the foregoing all refers to a very comprehensive menu, normally only found in a traditional and high-class restaurant. To bring us back to earth, a menu offering one soup, egg, sausage and chips, plaice and chips, cottage pie, ice cream or cheese, tea and coffee, is still technically an à la carte menu. It is a question of degree. Many of our large company operations do go in for a very simple menu structure, however, and it is a conscious marketing strategy. It can be undeniably successful if attractively executed and in the right trading position.

Table d'Hôte

The alternative to à la carte, although one can effectively offer a combination of both, is the table d'hôte menu consisting of a fixed number of courses at a fixed price. The courses can offer alternatives, and adjustments can be effected by the addition of supplementary prices in the case of certain more expensive dishes or extra courses. Whereas before the Second World War the four-course lunch and the six-course dinner were commonplace, three suffice nowadays for lunch and four for the dinner menu.

A typical lunch menu might offer a choice of say three items for the first course such as Soup of the Day, Fresh Melon or Spaghetti Bolognese. For the main course perhaps a fish dish, an entrée or two and a roast joint. Three or four vegetables including potatoes might be offered, and in the summer a cold meat dish and salad. Three or four sweets or a choice of cheese can conclude the menu. Coffee might be included according to the price structure although it is often charged for separately.

The dinner menu can be more elaborate with possibly a fish course included. People eating out in the evening are usually at leisure and can afford more time to relax over their meal. There is usually a tendency for the à la carte menu to be favoured in the evening although a fixed price table d'hôte is often a 'better buy' from a tourist's point of view. It is usual for the dinner menu to offer better-class dishes of a more expensive nature. Lunch-time customers are not only concerned with the short time in which they often have to take their meal but are more budget conscious too since it is something they have to consider every day possibly. Evening trade is different with the clients enjoying the company of friends and celebrating some occasion perhaps. Cost is not then such a critical consideration.

Order of Courses

The order of courses is the same as that for the à la carte menu and as follows: 1. Hors d'Oeurvre or Appetiser; 2. Soups; 3. Fish; 4. Entrée; 5. Roasts; 6. Sweets; 7. Cheese, or perhaps Savouries. For simplicity 1 and 2 can be combined, as can 4 and 5, and courses 6 and 7. Fresh fruit can also be offered as an alternative, or additional to, sweet or cheese. A pasta dish could be offered as an alternative to the fish course. Figures 3 and 4 show typical table d'hôte lunch and dinner menus.

Use of French Terms

People often ask why we use French in menus. Certainly we do not need to in a menu which is entirely English. Many of our classical dishes are of French origin and it is difficult to describe them otherwise except in lengthy detail. The menu should always be completely honest however. Unless it is technically possible to prepare and serve a classical French dish which is not a complete travesty of the original, it should be left alone.

A mixture of English and French is usually to be deplored. It is pretentious and bad examples can only tend to make a restaurant look foolish. The difficulty is, however, to give a named cut of fish, or meat say, its French garnish or method of cooking, and therefore often indicating its origins, without a mixture of languages. To give a possible example, it would be wrong to offer on the menu Roast Leg of Lamb Rôti à la Broche Boulangère. It should be either Gigot d'Agneau Rôti à la Broche Boulangère, or Spit-Roasted Leg of Lamb Boulangère (or Bakehouse) Style. In the first correct example the menu should be entirely in French or, in the second, completely in English. To assist clients it might be helpful to print in small type under the French (Roast Leg of Lamb garnished with Baked Sliced Potatoes and Small Onions).

Figure 3. *Typical table d'hôte lunch*

Chilled Fruit Juice Selection
Egg Mayonnaise
Spaghetti Bolognese
Cream of Chicken
***
Grilled Fillet of Plaice
with Tartare Sauce

Vol au Vent of Chicken
garnished with Asparagus

Roast Rib of Scotch Beef
Yorkshire Pudding

New Potatoes – Roast Potatoes
Spring Greens – Cauliflower Mornay
Buttered Baby Carrots
***
Caramel Cream
Blackcurrant and Apple Pie
with Double Cream
Bread and Butter Pudding
Ice Cream Selection
Cheese Board
***
Coffee

It is generally embarrassing to clients to be confronted with a menu written entirely in French. It is bad enough for them when they are abroad! It may give an establishment a 'swank' aura but it often means that the waiter is frequently consulted as to how the dish is prepared and garnished and this means having skilled and knowledgeable staff. If a client is entertaining too he does not like to display his ignorance in front of guests. However, this is a question of policy and if this is your

Figure 4. *Typical table d'hôte dinner*

Avocado Pear with Vinaigrette Sauce
Continental Sausage Selection
Clear Chicken Soup with Rice
Cream of Asparagus
***
Fresh Noodles in Butter and Parmesan

Poached Fillets of Lemon Sole
with Shrimp Sauce
***
Mixed Grill

Roast Duckling with Orange Sauce

Braised Stuffed Shoulder of Veal

French Fried, Roast or New Potatoes
Carrots Vichy Style   Baby Sprouts
Buttered French Beans
or
Cuts from the Cold Buffet
Ham, Ox Tongue, Roast Beef
with Assorted Salads
***
Peach Vacherin
Sherry Trifle with Cream
Coffee Gâteau
Ice Cream Selection
Cheese Board
***
Coffee

'scene' why not? Do things properly and ensure that methods and garnishes are authentic. Every garnish has some historic or geographic connection, or an association with a famous chef or personality. Clients who really do know what they are ordering are right to complain if a 'Sole Bonne Femme' comes to the table coated in a Béchamel Sauce with a few mushrooms in it! I have seen it happen in places that really should know better. Far better to serve an honest and well-cooked Grilled Dover Sole which is within the capabilities of the kitchen.

Trade Description Act

Remember that it is unlawful to serve any item which is described as something different. I am not associating this statement particularly with wrongly describing a French garnish: we are not so concerned with what might loosely be described as 'artistic interpretation' as with fact. You cannot serve Shoulder Ham for example if it is clearly shown on the menu as Gammon. They are from different ends of the pig and quite different in quality too! The law would not be broken if, in a sandwich, margarine was spread on the bread instead of butter, unless it was stated that butter was used in the making of the sandwich. To take perhaps another example, an 'escalope' is a slice of meat which is beaten out thinly in the shape of a large scallop shell, hence, its name. It is widely accepted that an escalope (or scallop) is usually of veal. However this need not be so. If you were to take a slice of raw turkey breast and treat it as veal served perhaps with an appropriate spaghetti garnish and described it as 'Escalope Milanese' you would probably be deceitful but not unlawful, unless you had described it as veal.

Please do not think I am encouraging you into sharp practice! The question of maintaining an honest trading policy has been emphasised enough I would hope. The foregoing has served purely to illustrate the implications. Restaurants have, on occasion, been heavily fined for serving mutton when they have described it as Roast Lamb. The Weights and Measures Inspector has power to demand to see invoices. The phrase 'not of the quality and substance demanded' may have a familiar ring. A great deal of emphasis is placed on 'consumer protection' and 'fair trading' these days.

Menu Padding

Beware of using what might be called 'menu padding'. To use an illustration or two – Grilled Cutlets of Southdown Lamb when it hailed from New Zealand, or Tay Salmon when it was last seen swimming up the Hudson River! It may well serve to glamourise the menu, but unless you want to risk your reputation by a court case well reported in the local news media, Grilled Lamb Cutlets or Poached Salmon, as the case may be, will have to do. One last example: if a 'five-course' menu is advertised, do not serve four courses of soup, fish, meat and sweet and show a fifth as 'After Eight Mints'. It will not wash. Even coffee is not a course in the accepted sense.

Banquet or Party Menus

Whilst most restaurants may not serve banquets a few words may be useful on the subject of parties. It is customary, and indeed necessary, to adopt the straight table d'hôte type menu where significant numbers are concerned. This is necessary to facilitate service. To offer very much choice would make planning difficult, service chaotic, and be wasteful of food. Whilst offering a choice of first course, say Melon or Soup, would not cause too much of a problem, it is customary and indeed wise to offer a completely straight menu thereafter. Obviously this depends on the size of the party and on being able to accommodate any special requirements of the organiser.

When arranging party menus there are certain essential factors to consider. The menu should not be so ambitious as to cause cooking, service or equipment problems. It is also necessary, because parties are often booked well in advance, to ensure that food supplies of any particular kind will in fact be available for the date in question.

Seasonability

Seasonability of foods is not quite such a factor as it once was. Not only the deep freeze, but the advent of air transport has meant that many foods which were once out of the question at certain times of the year are now often obtainable. There are, however, some foods which are strictly controlled by season-ability and these include items of game such as grouse, pheasant, partridge and the like, as well as oysters of course. Parties are often booked several months ahead so when quoting menus for such occasions, costing considerations apart, the menu must take full cognizance of the availability of whatever items are needed. It might be possible to obtain some foreign strawberries in February for example if one is well connected and near a major market, or is served by a wholesaler of repute. If there is doubt or risk, however, it would be safer not to quote. In any case the cost might be something of a shock. One does not ordinarily like to draw attention to the fact that an item must have been deep frozen and whilst it might be perfectly feasible to serve cold pheasant at a buffet in July it might well cause a few raised eyebrows. If challenged, one cannot say that it was shot a week or so ago! Let us just say that it is wiser and better to preserve some of our mystique and illusion.

Menu Balance

Balancing the menu is important where a straight table d'hôte is concerned. Balance, as such, in an à la carte menu obviously does not matter since it is the diner who chooses as he thinks unless he is advised, and it is therefore up to him. To some extent this also applies to the table d'hôte menu which offers alternatives. However, once the menu becomes inflexible there are certain rules to abide by. These are concerned not only with the gastronomic and digestive aspects, but with visual appeal as well.

Appearance

Visual appeal can be applied in two senses: the appearance of the particular dish in the balancing of colours, and then of the menu as a whole composition – the contrast on the plate and the contrast of course following course. An extreme example of lack of colour contrast might be Boiled Mutton and Caper Sauce, Mashed Potatoes and Turnips! An almost totally white meal and although perhaps with contrast of flavours devoid of visual interest. An example of poor menu composition, again only thinking in terms of colour would be a brown soup, deep-fried fish fillets, roast chicken, roast potatoes, braised celery and baked parsnips, followed by a chocolate type sweet. A decided predominance of brown! Composing a menu requires very considerable thought in this direction. There is nothing like an attractive dish, full of colour and with care taken over its presentation to awaken the taste buds. It is a gastronomic fact. We have all experienced it.

Digestive Considerations

Returning to digestive considerations these too are important, particularly if the menu is to consist of say, five or six courses which, whilst not so fashionable now, does occur on special occasions. Even with four courses there can easily be a tendency for too much richness, or perhaps too much starch. The inclusion of two pastry dishes should be avoided, say a Vol au Vent and then a flan or similar. Try to avoid potatoes with both the entrée and the roast course. If a rich sauce is to be served with the fish course then it would be better to serve a clear soup before it. Rich meats too, or those which tend to be fatty, should not follow each other such as Best End of Lamb or Pork and Goose. The reason why we serve sharp sauces such as Mint or Apple Sauce, etc., is to kill such richness which might upset a sensitive digestion. The composition should start with dishes which stimulate the palate and gradually increase the 'weight' of successive courses, concluding with a light sweet and/or savoury. The greater the number of courses, the smaller they should be of quantity and be more 'lightweight' in character. It is customary to serve a sorbet (or water ice) between the entrée and roast courses. This allows the meal to proceed in a more leisurely fashion and enables the diner to take a breather. Perhaps a cigarette can be taken with the chairman or host's permission; in which case tradition suggests Russian cigarettes as the correct form.

From the foregoing it will be seen that menu composition is much more complex perhaps than one would imagine. It is a subject which draws on total experience covering most of the skills of restaurant-keeping. It requires an appreciation of so many factors and there are many traps to fall into. Looking at the modern scene, unless one has the expertise and knowledge to operate a traditional and high-class restaurant the best advice is to keep menus as simple and as streamlined as possible, consistent with trading considerations. If labour is a problem, and more than likely it will be, then a fast food type menu, based on convenience foods mainly, will provide the answer. The emphasis being on quality of presentation rather than preparation requiring technical skill. As has been previously mentioned in another context, one can learn a great deal from studying the larger companies' operations and drawing inspiration and ideas. There is absolutely no reason why the small independent caterer should not operate in a similar way as long as he does not take them on at their own game next door!

CHAPTER 11

Party Organisation

Party organisation requires a very great deal of thought, planning and attention to detail. This is certainly one area where record keeping is essential and nothing should be left to memory or chance. There is nothing more horrific than a party which has been double booked or perhaps, for which the wrong menu has been prepared. All manner of things can go wrong which can result in trouble, chaos and disappointed and irate clients, unless every detail is carefully logged beforehand. Things can go wrong, of course, which are not always the fault of the caterer, such as non-delivery of specially ordered supplies.

However, clients too can sometimes can commit *faux pas* if they are not good organisers. They perhaps fail to notify final numbers, with the result that more guests arrive than food is prepared for, or covers laid. They have been known to get the date wrong on the invitations, or even the time. Their printers may miss a course out on the menu, which, whilst not too critical in itself, tends to make the restaurant look foolish. Guests nearly always tend to blame the establishment for such minor or major disasters instead of their host or organiser. How then should this problem be approached?

The Menu Selection

Oblique reference has already been made in Chapter 8 (Purchasing) to the question of supplies, particularly seasonability, etc., as has the compilation of menus for parties and banquets in Chapter 9. Assuming this is noted, it is now advisable to produce a selection of specially priced and constructed menus for functions. These should take into account all the factors that have been identified so far. However, quite apart from the supply angle, one must remember at all times the limitations of the equipment installed, such as hotplate storage, and of the ability of the kitchen to cope. Having such a selection of menus at hand means that when an enquiry is received it is possible to offer something immediately. This is not only time saving but businesslike. One can always mention to the client that such menus are only a guide as to what can be offered and that changes can be accommodated if required subject to possible price alterations, etc. At least there is a starting point. Emphasis should also be made that only one menu can be offered or you may be confronted with a request for a selection to cover the whole party!

Number of Courses

Menus can be either three, four or more courses, or can be basically three courses with, for example, a selection of separately priced fish courses. Some caterers offer separately priced courses and allow the client to build up his own menu but this is not always a good idea as it takes the control out of the caterer's hands and can result in some cheap and badly balanced menus. I would not recommend this approach. Keep as much control as possible, for you have got to prepare and serve the meal. If a client requests a course which you have doubts about in any way it is better to be honest and dissuade him than do a poor job. After all, you are there to advise. Remember too the question of what cutlery, crockery and glass as well as service equipment will be needed and ensure that you are sufficiently stocked. If it would appear that you will have to spend a capital sum on some special equipment, unless you are going to find it useful in the future, you could well make a loss on the function instead of a profit.

Master Work-Sheet

Having agreed on what is practicable, a start can be made on getting all the facts on paper. Whilst obviously changes can be made to take into account special requirements of your own, the illustration of a typical work-sheet will be found in Figure 5 and should be helpful in showing the detail needed. Make sure it is all faithfully recorded (date, time, etc.), and it is also always advisable to confirm the arrangements in writing to the customer and to receive similar confirmation that he accepts the arrangements made. Specify a date if possible for the final number to be advised or at least a figure that is reasonably near the mark. If special supplies have to be ordered and purchased which are not normally part of your menu structure this could result in either possible wastage or not having sufficient for the meal if the final number is very different from the original estimate; this often happens.

Table Arrangements

Functions are roughly what one might call formal or informal. A formal function might well require a 'top table' with the principal guests and speakers, or in the case of weddings, the bride and groom, parents, bestman and bridesmaids, etc., so arranged that they sit facing the other guests. The rest of the room may then either be arranged as sprigs off the top table or separate tables for eight or ten perhaps. Alternatively, an informal function may not require top table arrangements but only separate tables for specified numbers. Whatever arrangement the organiser requires should be defined and entered on the work-sheet. Be sure of course that the arrangement suggested or required is in fact a physical possibility. Experience will soon tell you what can be accomplished or not, but for the first occasion or two careful measurements should be taken or, if possible, the room laid out for a dummy run. Do not forget that service staff have to pass between sprigs when the chair has been pulled out. Trying to get a quart into a pint pot only makes for discomfort and frustration for all concerned so be practical, recognise what is a practical limit and stick to it. Tell the organiser what the absolute physical limit is and that it is not possible to cater for more. There are bound to be many occasions when you may have to turn a function away because it is too big.

Table Plans

It is not really the responsibility of the caterer to produce a table plan or type place cards. But certainly an outline of the table arrangements should be produced in rough with the places marked for the assistance of the client, and it is in your

Figure 5.   Master work-sheet for party organisation

DATE   No. of Guests
                                                      Approx.   Final Advice
                                    STAFF
NAME   BOOKED
ADDRESS

Telephone No.   Menu: Price: Service Charge
Type of Party

Timetable
Bar Arrangements

Service Facilities
Menus
Table Plan
Place Cards
Flowers
Taped Music
Licence Extension   Hire Charge
Photographer
Table Arrangements   Reception and Apéritifs

                                    Wines with Meal

                OFFICE USE
Aperitifs
Bar
Wines   Liqueurs
Food   Other Drinks
Service Charge   Cigarettes and Cigars
Exemption Order   Toasts, etc.
Cake Stand and Knife
                                    Any Special Service Requirements:

Overall Total
                    _____
                                    Render Account to:
              Notes
                                          Deposit   Date

                                    Date Enquiry   Client seen by

                                    Date Confirmation   Party confirmed by

interest to do so. If you do not then he may saddle you with something which is quite impractical. It is a question of liaison and co-operation to ensure that all goes well on the night. A small easel or stand to be provided for the display of the table plan in a prominent place is a useful piece of equipment to have if parties are a regular feature of the trade.

Deposits

The demanding or acceptance of a deposit is a question of house policy. It is not often that dinners are cancelled but it can happen. The caterer may feel he should protect himself. Weddings, however, regrettably get cancelled or sometimes postponed for a variety of reasons. Since they are invariably held on a Saturday afternoon, and are usually booked well in advance, it could well be that having taken a booking, the caterer will turn further bookings away. This often happens at popular periods of the year, such as Easter. The taking of a deposit in these circumstances is highly advisable in case of cancellation.

Wedding Bookings

When taking a wedding booking there is usually more detailed knowledge required than would be the case for say a dinner. There is the question of the cake for example. Who is supplying it? If you are not then when will it arrive? Is it square, round or what shape otherwise? If you are only supplying the stand you will want to know what shaped stand you need. If you are supplying the stand and knife you may wish to make a separate hire charge for it. You should specify this.

Flowers

With regard to flowers, it may be your policy to have plenty of fresh flowers around and this may be sufficient. Doting parents however may require special floral decorations. This will need to be clearly specified and charged for. Are they being sent in or does the caterer arrange them?

Wedding Breakfasts

As is the case of set menus for dinners, it is always wise to compile a few with a wedding breakfast in view. Dinners mostly take place in the winter or colder months, weddings mostly in spring, summer and autumn. The wedding menu, therefore, should have a lighter bias and possibly an emphasis on a salad-type main course, say salmon or chicken and ham and other cold meats, in one or two examples.

Buffets

Very often the most popular arrangement these days for a wedding reception is a buffet-type meal. This allows guests to mingle and is less formal and rigid, avoiding the need for table plans. There are two types of buffet, a 'finger buffet' and a 'fork buffet'. The former consists of food which, as the name suggests, is eaten with the fingers. Small dainty varieties of sandwiches, bridge rolls, bouchées, cheese straws, sausage rolls, chipolatas, cheese, etc., on sticks, small pastries, etc., being typical examples. On those rarer winter occasions, some of the food such as sausage rolls, chipolatas or perhaps Quiche Lorraine, can be served hot. Canapés could be offered to take with the apéritif on arrival and the buffet can be further bolstered by a sweet such as sherry trifle perhaps.

The 'fork' type of buffet is a slightly more substantial repast and consists of food which, in the correct context, should be able to be eaten standing up, with a fork as the only cutlery necessary. This has to be carefully planned and thought out since a good proportion of the meal will be either fish or meats in some form or the other. Very small attractively dressed pieces of 'fork' size should, therefore, be contemplated. The best form of salads to serve are those of a composite type such as potato, Russian, Spanish, coleslaw, etc., although cucumber and tomatoes in vinaigrette sauce are, of course, easy to manage. Quite imaginative catering can be carried out and an attractive fork buffet can be fun to produce. Once fish, such as salmon say, or joints of beef, ham, turkey, chicken, etc., are displayed and require carving and served with salads of lettuce or chicory, then a full service of cutlery becomes necessary. This type of meal is often more of a labour of love than a full-scale dinner. The only difference from a service standpoint being that the guest will transport his own food from the buffet to the table. Tables can either be laid in the usual way or the cutlery necessary for the entire meal wrapped in a serviette and picked up when the first course is collected. Service staff usually clear dirty plates when the diner leaves his place to collect his next course.

Coffee is usually served whatever the type of buffet and this is brought to the table.

Service of the Cake

Once the champagne (or other wine) has been poured for the toast, the bottom tier of the cake is removed to a convenient place and cut into fingers for service. It is then served to guests when the speeches are concluded. This procedure takes place after coffee has been served in the case of a seated meal, but in the event of a buffet it is tidier to leave the coffee service until afterwards.

Wines

When the booking is made it is always advisable, if at all possible, to try to get a decision about the choice of wines. This will enable you to ensure not only sufficient stocks but that it can be served at the correct temperature. Whilst this is usually possible where weddings or hosted functions are concerned, one often finds that wines are ordered at the table in the case of a 'ticket' dinner. One just has to be prepared for anything!

Staff

Using one's regular staff as a foundation, the customary arrangement is to establish contact with waitresses in the locality who are prepared to work on a casual basis. These are known as 'extras'. It is, of course, necessary to book these as far in advance as possible as there is often a heavy demand for their services by hotels in the area. Having booked the required number according to the 'services' of the function, a note should be made on the work-sheet of their names for reference. They will, of course, be informed of the time they are required to assist in laying up, etc. Transport home may be needed should the function be late at night and this should be arranged if necessary. Payment of such 'extras' is very often a question of whatever the going rate is locally and this can be considerably higher than the statutory rate depending on local competition. In addition they customarily receive a share of the service charge.

Miscellaneous Detail

Most of the essential basic detail has been dealt with but there are always special instructions the host or organiser may wish to give. He may well forget at the time of making the booking to mention these and it is as well to jog his memory. The kind of information that is needed is perhaps whether liqueurs are to be served or offered. If so, are these to be on a cash basis or charged to account? This seems simple enough, but if not known can result in awkwardness at the time of service or perhaps a bill that the host did not want or had not budgeted for. Does he wish cigars or cigarettes to be offered? If yours is the type of restaurant with a small dance floor and a band is to play for the function you would want to know whether meals, drinks, or sandwiches are required for the musicians.

Exemption Order

Whilst this subject will be more fully dealt with in a subsequent chapter, it is essential to know if liquor is to be consumed on the premises outside licensing hours, assuming of course that the premises are licensed! If the function is to be held during the afternoon, such as a wedding, or late at night as in the case of a dinner-dance, then an exemption order will most certainly be needed. This requires a letter to you from the host, or organiser, asking you to apply to the magistrates on his behalf. As a time scale is involved for such applications it is essential to deal with this as soon as possible.

The client invariably writes a letter which is far from what is needed either omitting essential detail or perhaps including much information which is of no interest to the magistrates or the police. It is, therefore, a good idea to run off on a duplicator a standard type letter (see Figure 6). All that is necessary is to fill in details when the client has signed it, and send it with a covering letter to the clerk to the magistrates.

Toasts and Presentations

A gavel and block is an essential piece of table furnishing if there are likely to be speeches. The client should be asked if this is likely to be the case. If the function is formal, it will almost certainly be. A note should be made on the work-sheet. Similarly bouquets are sometimes presented as a surprise at perhaps the coffee stage. In this situation you may be asked to be the custodian of them until required. It will be necessary to know this or you may wonder, on receipt of a bouquet or two, who they are intended for – particularly if you have more than one function on the go.

Figure 6. *Suggested format for exemption order application (client to restaurateur)*

Name and address
of the restaurant
Dear Sir,

Re: *(State function and date)*

I should be grateful if you would apply to the Licensing Justices for an exemption order permitting consumption of liquor in the (name of the restaurant) from   until
on the above date on the occasion of (state type of function).

Yours faithfully,
(Signed by applicant)
(Print name)
(Address of applicant)

Telegrams, etc.

Another quandary one sometimes meets, if more than one party or wedding is taking place, is to receive telegrams or letters addressed by Christian names only. The function is booked in the bride's maiden name or family name too. Telegrams or letters may arrive for the bride and groom whose name is, of course different, If you do not have a note of this it can be awkward perhaps. Telegrams and letters are placed near to the wedding cake, or on the top table near the best man's place.

Payment

The work-sheet should contain details of any deposit paid and when, whether the account is to be sent and, of course, to whom.

Finally it is very useful to have a telephone number where you can make contact with the host or party organiser. Sometimes they can be very lax in notifying final numbers or even their choice of menu should these have been sent or taken away. It is all part and parcel of having everything sewn up. Getting down on paper every single detail is all part of smooth organisation and a trouble-free function. It does not take long and can save a large number of headaches in the long run.

Internal Distribution

Having completed a total picture of the party's requirements, the office knows what is required but it is still necessary to pass the information on to those departments who are to do the job. In this connection good communications are needed. How elaborate these are, of course, is a question of how complex the organisation is. In a large business there are many more departments that would be concerned in providing services from the florist to the cellar. However, this is hardly likely in a small to medium restaurant where the proprietor has much more intimate and close control. The chef will most certainly need to be advised however, and whoever is in charge of the dining room and wines. Those details which concern them should, therefore, be notified, such as date, time, numbers of covers, menu, wines and other drinks, number of services and so on. If parties are a regular feature of one's trade, a monthly list of known commitments can be circulated so that staffing can be arranged satisfactorily.

Final Comment

Functions can be a lucrative source of revenue and, if properly executed can be very good advertising. After all a large number of guests may come to your establishment for the first time and if they go away suitably impressed will come back again for a meal on their own or with friends. They will certainly talk about the function, that is for sure, so do it well. Doing it well means being properly organised and being prepared for all eventualities. Preparing 'services' of food gives rein to imagination and careful preparation and, since the food is the same for all the guests, is often easier than a busy evening serving a multiplicity of orders. Good timing is essential in the kitchen, however, particularly in the case of vegetables and other foods which do not keep well. Good communications and liaison with the dining room are a prerequisite therefore.

CHAPTER 12

Staffing and Legislation

Recruitment

Obtaining staff not only of sufficient quantity, but of trained quality, is, and has been for some years, one of the caterer's main problem areas. What is being done? The hotel and catering departments of the technical colleges offer many courses in craft, supervisory and management technique. Having completed these courses the students leave college every summer to seek employment in the industry. Recognising the shortage of skilled and trained staff, the government caused the Hotel and Catering Industry Training Board to be set up in 1967 with the aim of raising standards, introducing effective and viable training schemes for workers and, in the process, taking over the functions of the old National Joint Apprenticeship Council. In more recent times the government has introduced such retraining schemes as the 'Training Opportunities Scheme' and 'Limited Skills' in order to try to attract redundant workers from other industries. The Employment Service Dept. also set up specialised Employment Bureaux for the industry at strategic points around the country. The industry itself has also, through its trade associations, paid considerable attention to the problem of recruitment through the publication of information leaflets, a pilot study, and the sponsorship of

careers conventions, school talks, etc. In short, much effort
has gone into attracting workers into the industry. It must still,
however, be the responsibility of each caterer to plan his staffing requirements intelligently.

Needs of the Business

How the trading policy is planned in the first instance will
constitute a major factor in deciding the staffing needs. When
starting a new business, assessing and recognising the local
employment situation can help considerably. Very often the
'situations vacant' columns in the local newspaper will give an
indication of the shortages and the demand. If, therefore, in a
specific area it is known that staffing is particularly difficult, the
trading policy should be one of simplicity and the operation's
staffing needs commensurate. A complicated and extensive
high-class menu will, of course, require skilled operatives both
in the kitchen and the restaurant itself. It is, for example,
easier to obtain an unskilled or semi-skilled woman who can
be quickly trained to give plate service than to obtain a highly
skilled waitress or waiter capable of silver service and lamp
work, etc. Similarly in the kitchen where the preparation of
classical dishes would demand a brigade of trained craftsmen.
Recognition of this fact has emerged already in preceding
chapters. Not only will the quality of staff be affected by the
policy decision, of course, but so will be the numbers to be
employed. Other factors too which will influence the decisions
are the trading hours and whether staff are to be predomin-
antly full time or part time. Often it is a case of getting what
one can and filling the staffing gaps as effectively as possible!
It may be more economical to use part-time staff only to
supplement at known peak periods.

Means of Recruitment

Traditionally it has usually been the policy to advertise locally
for living-out staff, or in the case of living-in staff through the
national press (trade press or others) and through the agencies.
Agencies, of course, require a fee, often one week's wages, but

this varies. If engaging through an agency it is advisable to be particularly thorough in vetting applicants. Invariably there is no refund if the person engaged subsequently turns out to be useless! Apart from the famous Denmark Street Catering Staff Bureau in London, the Department of Employment was not in the past much favoured by the industry for solving staff problems. However, following lobbying by the B.H.R.C.A., the trade's national association, the Employment Service Dept. has recently set up some twenty specialised hotel and catering staff bureaux already referred to. Any vacancies should, therefore, be notified to them and they will do their best to help. If there is not such a bureau immediately locally, the local E.S.A. office will put you in touch or will automatically pass the vacancy on. This service is growing and is very useful. It is useful too to establish a link with the local technical college head of department who will perhaps have catering students who require placing at the end of term, or even for industrial experience during their course.

Foreign Workers

Since our involvement in the E.E.C., the considerable barriers which existed against employing nationals from those countries have eased. There is, however, just as great a shortage of skilled operatives on the continent as there is here. Often the only attraction to come to the U.K. is to learn our language unless there are other inducements such as a high salary, but wage levels are often higher elsewhere in Europe. In any case living-in accommodation is almost certainly required. Advertising in the foreign press and contact with the agencies is the usual recruitment procedure.

As far as other foreign staff resident outside the Common Market are concerned, the number allowed to work here is strictly controlled. Application should be made to the Home Office when work permits may only be granted in exceptional circumstances. Even if you are successful there may be travelling expenses to face and, once here, there is no hold on the worker to remain with you; having obtained his work permit, he can move on. There could also well be a language difficulty of course.

Trainee Schemes

Whilst it is taking the long-term view, entering into one or more of the trainee schemes operated by our training board does much to help, but it is not something which can be entered into lightly. The Hotel and Catering Industry Training Board will, in the first instance, need to be satisfied that the establishment will be able to offer training expertise and that the kind of work carried on will give the trainee the opportunity to develop. This means that the restaurant will first have to seek and obtain approval by the Board. It will also mean that some departmental senior staff in the business will have to complete a Board-approved Trainer Skills Course, and be registered. Trainees will be required to follow an approved training plan of development and be day-released to technical college once a week during term-time. This all adds up to a considerable responsibility. However, many small establishments do operate successful training schemes and, being members of their local Training Groups, have found the experience rewarding and indeed often contributing to their own development and efficiency as well as attracting grants.

Craft Courses

Most small establishments are only interested in the courses leading to craft qualifications, i.e. cooks and waiters or waitresses. Trainee cooks usually follow a training programme in two parts of two years each. The first two years are spent studying for the City & Guilds Certificate in Basic Cookery No. 706/1 and this can be followed by a further year of study for the attainment of the City & Guilds 706/2, Cookery for the Catering Industry. Trainee waiters/waitresses can take a one year course, the City & Guilds 707/1 Food Service Certificate. It is, of course, possible to follow up with more advanced courses for further professional development such as the City & Guilds 706/3 Advanced Professional Cookery, 707/2 for more advanced service techniques, and 717 Alcoholic Beverages Certificate.

Whilst, of course, it is perfectly true that one cannot expect to keep youngsters after they have finished their training, many do stay for a year or two and this allows a trained staff to be built up whilst others take their place under training. Grants are paid by the Hotel and Catering Industry Training Board towards training costs for such trainees on day release. Levy is paid by the larger employers although properly planned training programmes are recognised by the Board and will lead to levy exemption. Due to the pay-roll level laid down by the Board, it is hardly likely that a small employer will be liable for levy nowadays. The usual source from which to obtain trainees straight from school is the careers officer of the local Education Committee, or by advertising in the local news media. Care should be taken to ensure that young people subsequently interviewed are properly motivated and are fully aware of what is involved. Often they may have had some holiday or Saturday working experience in a hotel or restaurant. It is a good idea to try to encourage youngsters to do this kind of holiday work, but do read your local by-laws first. Quite often such local laws prohibit young people from working in our industry or, even if they do not, the permitted hours of work are stringent. An establishment does not necessarily have to be registered by the H.C.I.T.B. for its staff to be permitted to attend technical colleges. However, it would not be possible to obtain grant.

Engaging Staff

With the current shortage of trained staff, there is sometimes the tendency to engage anyone who comes along! Selection is, of course, very important, particularly if the business is concerned with maintaining a high standard and a good reputation. When one is desperate and has perhaps tried to recruit for weeks on end without success, it is not an easy matter to turn an applicant away, however substandard. Yet, if it is obviously courting trouble to engage such an applicant, it is not common sense to do so. Even a dishwash-machine operator turning out substandard work can lead to complaints of dirty cutlery, crockery or glass. The service staff are then given a great deal of extra work of polishing, and either become discontented or allow things to 'go' when under pressure. A cook who burns and wastes food, or serves food which is inedible, is plainly more of a liability than an asset, as is a waiter or waitress who is surly and unkempt.

Vetting the Applicant

The taking up and checking of references is, therefore, an important and first step. Except in the case of long-serving staff who leave of their own volition, the practice of providing a written reference has largely disappeared. It should, however, always be possible to ask for details of previous employers and to telephone them asking for details of length of service, quality of performance and particularly the reason for leaving that employment. The applicant may have been dismissed for stealing, or even for hitting a customer with a teapot! You cannot tell without checking and thus safeguarding yourself. The often volunteered information that he or she has worked 'here and there, and everywhere', should be treated with caution, particularly if the jobs have been in rapid succession. It is always advisable to ask a few technical questions such as how the applicant would prepare or serve a certain dish or sauce. Enquire too into the domestic background and, in the case of a married woman, whether the husband has been fully consulted about his wife's prospective employment. Employment of staff expected to work late or awkward hours may present a travelling problem; check this out.

Applicants for a part-time situation may already have a 'first employment' in which case the income tax position may be affected. It is dangerous to assume that all part-time employees can be treated as 'casual' labour. If they work regularly, say a set number of mornings or evenings per week, then they cannot by any stretch of imagination be classed as 'casual'. It is, therefore, always wise to notify Inland Revenue of the circumstances and to follow their instructions.

Staff Records

It is valuable to maintain a record sheet for every member of staff engaged. It represents a dossier if you like on each employee and should cover every facet of the span of employment. Figure 7 shows the kind of information to be recorded. When the employee leaves, the record should be filed and kept for future reference. It is surprising how often one has to refer to it in such cases as claims for unemployment benefit for example, and it is useful to be able to refer to it when supplying information to another employer subsequently.

Figure 7. *Staff engagement form and working record*

Name	Address	Previous employ-ers	N.H.I. number Rate of contribu-tion
			P.45 received
Position offered: Wage:	Date commenced work	Reason for leaving	
			P.45 returned
Contract form signed	Date finished work	Pay increases	Tax coding
Miscellaneous	Character assess-ment		Amended coding

H.C.I.T.B. Courses   H.C.I.T.B. Grant received

Date and duration of holidays				Date and duration of sickness/absence				
Entitlement	From	Till	Days If taken paid	From	Till	Medical cert.	If paid	Illness

N.B. – When entering dates, these should be inclusive (first and last day).

Legislation that affects Staff

Once staff are employed the amount of administration required by legislation is considerable. In the early 1970s, successive governments vied with each other to produce more and more Acts of Parliament and Orders to protect the employee. We are not, however, concerned with political arguments, but with the effect this has on the small business from an administrative standpoint. It is all too easy to be in ignorance of what is, after all, the law; but as we are frequently told, this is no excuse.

To those who are considering setting up in business, therefore, the following legislation should be studied with care. Regulations do change in detail, or are amended, quite frequently according to which way the political wind is blowing and to quote verbatim those which apply at the time of writing would mean that this chapter would probably become quickly out of date. It is, therefore, proposed to deal with the various acts only in broad outline of intent. The relevant government departments all issue up-to-date pamphlets or booklets free of charge and are usually helpful with advice in any case.

Contracts of Employment

Contracts of employment legislation is now covered by the Employment Protection (Consolidation) Act, 1978 which repealed the Contracts of Employment Act, 1972. The effect is to protect employees by means of a written 'statement' of certain terms of their employment. The employer is required to issue a statement of such terms and it must be given within 13 weeks of an employee starting work. Some exceptions are employees working less than 16 hours per week, or 8 hours if they have worked for the same employer for the past 5 years. Such a statement need not be signed unless the employer wishes the statement to become a contract. In which case *all* the conditions should be stated.

In essence, the statement should contain the following: names and addresses of both parties; date on which employment started; scales and calculation of pay, and at what intervals; holiday pay and entitlement; conditions relating to sickness or injury; the period of notice of termination on both sides (minimum periods being laid down by law). The statement must also refer to the existence of a pension scheme, if any, giving details of rights, contributions, etc. and it must state whether a 'contracting out' certificate (Social Security Pensions Act, 1975) is in force or not. It should also state if a previous employment counts as being 'continuous', and the date on which such employment started. A 'job title' should be specified. The statement should also refer to disciplinary rules and grievance procedures. The statement or contract need not be stamped. The content of the statement can be considerably shortened by making reference to official documents (i.e. Wages Regulations) but these must be freely available for staff to see.

In addition to the foregoing, the Employment Protection Act also covers the subjects of redundancy and unfair dismissal. It is an important Act which employers need to have a sound knowledge of.

Offices, Shops and Railway Premises Act, 1963

This act came into being mainly to provide for the safety,

health and welfare of staff. Catering premises such as restaurants, cafés, etc., are regarded as shops and so come within
the scope of the act. Only premises in which self-employed
persons and their immediate relatives work are excluded from
the provisions of the act, otherwise any owner or occupier is
held to be legally liable to comply. Premises used only tem-
porarily, such as non-permanent structures, are also excluded
up to a period of six months.

The premises have to be notified and registered to the local
authority and a special form of application can be obtained
from them for this purpose.

The Act covers quite a range of facilities and working conditions and, like most legislation, needs to be studied carefully.
Requirements covered include overcrowding of workers in a
room, a kitchen if you like, where this would be considered a
risk to health and a possible cause of injury. Whilst principally
directed at offices, it requires reasonable temperatures to be
maintained, 16° C. (60.8° F.) after the first hour, and a thermo-
meter to be provided to check the temperature. Quite obviously kitchens and cold rooms, etc., have to be considered in a
special context and the Act would appear to allow a certain
flexibility. However, ventilation must be 'effective'.

Sanitary Conveniences

Other requirements are the provision of proper and sufficient
sanitary conveniences and washing facilities so that hygiene
can be safeguarded. Hot and cold running water and soap
must be provided, plus suitable means of drying. Such facilities
must be kept in a clean and orderly condition. The number of
toilets and urinals is laid down in a scale which was introduced
in 'The Sanitary Conveniences Regulations' of 1964. See also
'The Washing Facilities Regulations 1964'.

Dangerous Machines

The Prescribed Dangerous Machine Order 1964 makes it
obligatory for employers to see that any employee required to
operate any of the listed machines – for example, slicers,
chopping bowls, chippers, etc. – is fully instructed and trained

in their use and in the precautions to be taken. Safety guards must be properly fixed and in use.

Posters are required to be displayed so that staff may be familiar with the Act generally or a booklet be readily accessible to them.

Inspection

Inspectors are, of course, empowered to enter the premises at any time to see that the provisions of the acts are being complied with. They may interview staff and ask relevant questions. The proprietor of course has the right to demand proof of the inspector's official status.

Wages Regulations

What should the staff be paid? The question here is not so much of what the 'going rate' might be depending on local wages competition, but of the legal minimum scale specified by the Wages Council. The catering industry has for very many years now been subject to Wages Regulations. These specify minimum rates of pay, working hours and rest periods, holiday entitlement, as well as differing rates for workers taking meals on duty or living in.

There are principally two sets of regulations which could apply to cafés and restaurants, depending on whether they are licensed or not. The first are those known as L.R. (Licensed) and the others as U.P.R. (Unlicensed Place of Refreshment). The wages and conditions laid down in each case are in many respects quite different and it is not, therefore, feasible or lawful to use the U.P.R. regulations for a licensed establishment or vice versa.

The Office of Wages Councils, 12 St James's Square, London, SW1Y 4LL, is responsible for sending out in the first instance 'Proposals' which are usually in 'green paper' form informing employers of certain proposed changes in scales of wages or perhaps benefits. This gives all those concerned an opportunity to object within a certain period to such proposals. When finally the proposed alterations are settled a new and numbered order becomes effective from a certain date.

Both proposals and regulations must be posted up for staff to see.

To mention existing scales would be pointless since they change once a year. When starting a new business the proprietor should get in touch with the Wages Council at the address given above. Wages Inspectors do, of course, call periodically to check that the regulations are being adhered to. It is necessary to keep records in some form, either rotas of work, or a rather detailed wages book perhaps, to show what hours were worked in each case and particularly when and at what time of day. Spread-over rates and those for overtime are also specified. Work on public holidays, of course, is subject to particular scrutiny and involves extra payment and/or time off in lieu.

The country is split up into two areas for purposes of definition and the scales of pay differ in such areas from one to another. Area 'A' for example being the Metropolitan Police district, area 'B' being the rest of the country.

Whilst the existing regulations require careful study they are not too fearsome once understood. They are important, however, and every caterer should endeavour to familiarise himself with them.

Health and Safety at Work Act, 1974

This is an important piece of legislation which imposes obligations on an employer for all employees, and is binding on the self-employed. In broad terms, the Act, which was introduced in 1974 as an 'enabling' measure, has, as its aims, the following:

(i)   Securing the health, safety and welfare of persons at work.
(ii)   Protecting others from risks arising from work premises or activities.
(iii)   Controlling the storage and use of dangerous substances, e.g. inflammable or explosive substances.
(iv)   Controlling emission of noxious or offensive substances into the atmosphere.

Although the Act started to take effect from April 1975, regulations have since been made under it, for example the

Notification of Accidents and Dangerous Occurrences Regulation, 1980 and the Health and Safety (First Aid) Regulations, 1981, the latter coming into effect in July 1982. Pamphlets on the various aspects of the provisions of the Act are available from the Health and Safety Executive but it should be noted that the 'enforcing authority' is the Environmental Health Officer of the Local Authority and a great deal of time can be saved by approaching him direct. It is required that an employer furnishes his employees with a statement of policy under the Act.

Fire Precautions

Restaurants and cafés are concerned with the Fire Precautions Act where more than twenty people are employed at any one time, or more than ten, other than on the ground floor. In such cases a Fire Certificate is required from the local Fire Officer. Proper means of escape and the provision of adequate fire-fighting equipment of an approved type will have to be provided as well as attention to doors and other matters, as the Fire Officer may direct under the Act. Alarm bells and pushes will have to be provided at strategic points. Even from this brief look it will be seen that, when applicable, considerable expenditure is involved in bringing an establishment up to the required standard under the law. When buying a business therefore, it would be wise to check the position.

The Equal Pay Act

The object of this Act is to eliminate discrimination between the sexes as far as pay, opportunity and conditions of employment are concerned. It establishes the right of women to equal treatment when carrying out work which is broadly similar to that done by men in a like work-situation. However, even if the job is different, if it has been given a similar value in the context of 'job evaluation', the provisions and intent of the Act still apply.

Other Legislation

The Sex Discrimination Act, 1975 Effectively, this makes

sex discrimination unlawful, when engaging staff and offering
certain terms of employment. It covers both men and women
alike and in such areas as marital status, etc., and in the field of
training, opportunity, and promotion. Care needs to be exercised when wording advertisements for personnel, the word
'person' having taken on a new connotation!

The Race Relations Act, 1976   In addition to the foregoing,
racial discrimination in employment is similarly unlawful. In
offering employment there must be no hint of prejudice by
way of race or colour, or in selection and appointment,
opportunity or advancement. There must be no segregation
nor should an employer in any way show less favourable
treatment to an employee because of his or her ethnic origin.

The Shops Act   A restaurant or café is a 'shop' within the
meaning of the Act, and staff, even those working behind the
scenes, are technically shop assistants. The provisions of the
Shops Act should not be confused with the Catering Wages
Regulations. The former makes it compulsory for an employer to give his staff rest days and observe other conditions,
whereas the latter lays down minimum rates that must be
paid. Hence the confusion that often arises. The Shops Act
also covers weekly half-days (caterers have alternatives),
Sunday work, intervals for meals, etc., in addition to provisions covering young workers.

*Price Marking (Food and Drink on Premises) Order,
1979*   In essence, it is an offence for a restaurant or café,
whether giving table or offering cafeteria service, not to display its prices where a prospective customer cannot study
them before entering the premises. Displays of food and
drink prices (i.e. menus, etc.) should always be in a conspicuous place at, or very near to, the entrance. Prices must include
V.A.T., if applicable, and service or other extra charges
clearly shown. The Order is administered by the local
Weights and Measures Inspector.

CHAPTER 13

The Licensed Restaurant

Licensing Background and The Law

Since the main licensing laws were changed in 1961 it has been a comparatively easy matter for a restaurant to obtain a liquor licence within certain prescribed limits.. If one wishes to operate a better class of business it is really necessary to become licensed since such facilities are expected by the public; the disadvantages are few.

With the growth of tourism more and more visitors are coming to our shores. On the Continent, where many of them may come from, licensing arrangements are generally much looser than in Great Britain where even Wales and Scotland are somewhat different and more restrictive than England. All this is a source of bemusement to the continentals who find it difficult to understand why it is unlawful to have a drink in the afternoon or even on a Sunday in parts of Great Britain. There has been considerable pressure on government in recent years to allow relaxation of the licensing laws, the Errol Report having made many recommendations but to no avail. This is merely mentioned to illustrate that changes of law regarding liquor sales could take place in the enlightened future. It would be more realistic perhaps to deal in broad outline with those main points which are pertinent at present, and to look at what responsibilities, advantages or disadvantages there are in becoming licensed.

165

Qualifications for a Restaurant Licence

The applicant must have a good character and have not been barred from holding a liquor licence previously. The restaurant will have to qualify in several ways. The premises need to satisfy the Fire Officer that they are safe, that suitable means of escape and fire-fighting equipment exist. If they do not so satisfy his criteria he can very effectively block the application in court. The point here is that whilst plans have to be produced to the Licensing Justices, they themselves are not interested in the fire-safety aspect. It is, therefore, wise to seek the Fire Officer's advice before applying or you may leave court feeling disappointed.

The restaurant must offer a menu which contains food of a substantial nature. This precludes a café offering only light snacks from holding a licence. A copy of the menu has to be produced in court to satisfy the bench of its content. There must not be an undue element of teenage patronage and the premises must be suitably adapted. The police will visit the restaurant before the hearing to satisfy themselves that the premises are properly conducted and of sufficient repute.

Once the foregoing requirements have been satisfactorily met, the application may be proceeded with either at the Annual Licensing Meeting, or at a Transfer Sessions.

Procedure

A solicitor will, of course, be needed to carry through all the necessary procedures, and preferably one who specialises in such applications. Not less than twenty-one days before the Licensing Sessions, the applicant must give written notice to the Clerk to the Licensing Justices, the local Chief of Police and to the appropriate local authority as well as to the local fire authority. A plan of the premises is deposited with the Justices Clerk. Then, not more than twenty-eight days before the sessions, he must display notice of application for a period of one week at the premises which are to be licensed, usually on the restaurant window or anywhere where it can be seen and read by the public. A notice of application must also be inserted in the local newspaper not more than twenty-eight days or less than fourteen days before the Licensing Sessions. The solicitor, of course, will arrange all this. It is then customary for the applicant to appear in person on the day of the hearing in court. The procedure gives ample opportunity for any interested party to object to the granting of a licence. There is not usually much opposition these days to a restaurant licence, as long as all the requirements are being met. A full on-licence would be rather different.

The restaurant licence only permits liquor to be served to anyone taking a bona fide meal. It does allow an apéritif to be taken prior to the meal, and say liqueurs afterwards in a room ancillary to the dining room however, and as long as a 'substantial' meal is going to be, or has been, consumed. There are weaknesses, for perhaps a prospective diner might order a drink, consume it, and then decide not to eat! The law will have been broken; but in the main the system works well enough.

Licensing Hours

The hours of consumption are laid down for the area by the local Licensing Justices. These vary from say, the Metropolitan area to outlying districts. As long as the restaurateur does not permit consumption outside such dictated hours he need not stay open as late as public houses and has freedom to open and close when he wishes. He is not obliged to stay open for seven days per week, for example, as does a publican. Licensed establishments are, of course, subject to stricter supervision and control than unlicensed ones. Police make an annual inspection to see that everything is properly run. Weights and Measures Inspectors can call to check on the accuracy of optics used, that the statutory notices concerning size of measures being sold are being displayed, and that tankards, etc., conform to legislation.

Wage Rates

The licensed restaurant will be subject to a different scale of wage rates and conditions as mentioned in Chapter 12. On changing from an unlicensed situation, therefore, it will be

necessary to obtain copies of the L.R. Regulations and conform to them. It is, however, true to say that whilst formerly
wages rates and other conditions were substantially different,
particularly with regard to wages, compared with unlicensed
establishments, recent awards have seen a general levelling up.
The principal differences now are mainly in 'spreadover' rates
of payment for hours of duty.

Service Points

Details of the liquor service points will have to be disclosed on
the plan submitted to the Licensing Justices. It is not legally
necessary to have a bar as such and service might be effected
from a dispense hatch. Should there be sufficient space, however, it is very desirable to have a lounge bar where customers
may take a drink whilst looking at the menu or waiting for
their table. They may also take coffee and liqueurs there subsequently. This is what is meant by the words 'ancillary to the
dining room'. This is a convenient place in which to take the
client's order so that they may be called when their table and
first course is ready for service. There is no doubt that such
facilities effectively help sales of liquor too.

Supper Hour Certificate

It is possible to apply for a 'Supper Hour Certificate' which
allows drinks to be ordered and consumed for one hour after
the normal licensing hours in the district. For example should
local public houses close at 10.30 p.m., this would enable the
restaurant to serve drinks at the table until 11.30 p.m., to cover
those customers who are dining late. As restaurants are
allowed thirty minutes drinking-up time, as opposed to ten
minutes in a public house, this would mean that glasses should
be cleared from the table by midnight in this particular
instance.

It is also interesting to note that the Supper Hour Certificate
can give authority for drinks to be served for half an hour
after normal lunch-time drinking ceases. It is, however, necessary to inform the police of the restaurant's intention to do
this. This is particularly useful in the case of tourists or in the

better class business-type restaurant. It is, therefore, a wise foresight to apply for a certificate when applying for the restaurant licence. It is then permanently attached and does not have to be reapplied for on a renewal basis as does the main licence at the annual Brewster Sessions, when the yearly licensing fee is paid.

Exemption Orders

In the context of organisation, the subject of obtaining an 'Exemption Order' was referred to in Chapter 11. As will have been seen from the foregoing sections it is unlawful to serve liquor at any time outside what are known as 'permitted hours', i.e. the hours laid down for the area by the Licensing Justices plus the Supper Hour Certificate if you possess one. For any function at all that requires service of liquor outside such hours, it is necessary to obtain what is known as an Exemption Order. This, if granted, exempts the licensee from the restrictions. A letter (see Chapter 11 for the format) must be sent to the Licensing Justices and to the police. The time scale varies from area to area, but commonly the application must be made at least forty-eight hours before the weekly sessions take place. If the function is more than one month away then the application may be made by post which obviates the necessity to appear personally in court. However, do check with the Clerk to the Justices as to what local procedure is.

Currently the cost of an exemption order is £4.00, although this amount covers a block number of applications, if need be. There is a possibility, however, that should an advance application be made for an exemption order after the Annual Brewster Sessions, it might not be granted because it would presuppose the licence renewal. The Order would be needed in cases where drinking is to take place say in the afternoon or late at night in the case of a dinner-dance. This is known as a 'special occasion'. It is important to remember that it can only be applied for on behalf of a client who has specifically requested you to do so; it cannot be on your own behalf to extend your hours of operation.

Outside Catering and Occasional Licence

If you wish to concern yourself with outside catering and you are required to supply liquor on premises other than in the restaurant such as, say, the village hall or similar place, or perhaps in a marquee, then it is possible to do so. It will, however, be necessary to apply to the Licensing Justices for the granting of an 'Occasional Licence' which will then enable you to do this.

A Substantial Meal

What constitutes a 'substantial meal' in the eyes of the law is, to say the least, a very contentious issue! The spirit of the Act means what it says and it is generally accepted that it should be a meal of a reasonably substantial nature and eaten with a knife and fork. However, having made this point, one comes up against all manner of arguments and, in the end, it is a question of local interpretation. Certainly a snack meal, such as something on toast and on its own, does not really qualify in the strict sense of the wording, although it may well be eaten with a knife and fork. This is why the Justices like to see a copy of the menu before the granting of a licence.

The author was refused an exemption order on one occasion when an application was made for a buffet wedding. Since the buffet was of the 'finger' variety it did not constitute a 'substantial meal' in the eyes of the Clerk to the Justices. Subsequently special conditions were attached to my licence covering the point for the future.

Licence Transfer

Should a licensed restaurant be purchased then it will be necessary to arrange for the liquor licence to be transferred from the existing holder to the purchaser. The same qualifications of good character will apply, of course, in the case of the transferee, as they would were the application to be original. At least two references must be supplied to the police who will take them up. Whilst a temporary authority can be given by the police and the Clerk to the Justices, a transfer can only normally take place at a Licensing Sessions and notice of intention must be served on the police, the Justices Clerk and the local authority at least twenty-one days before the hearing. A competent solicitor will, of course, handle matters and, as long as the character is proved sound, there should not be any difficulties.

Supply

Having successfully obtained one's licence there comes the question of supply. This must to a large extent be related to the amount of business being done or envisaged. Liquor stocks can involve a great deal of capitalisation if a wide range is to be carried, and in a sufficient quantity. Once again it comes back to a policy decision based on the class and style of the business and one can only generalise. In a fast food operation the liquor sales can be simplified so that only bare essentials are sold. House wine in three or four types and sold only by the glass or carafe for example, or two types of sherry 'from the wood'. In this case make sure the cask is in fact wood and not plastic or you will be effectively contravening the 'description' legislation.

If the restaurant is traditional in character then a full range of apéritifs will have to be carried, a wine list giving a reasonable choice of the main types, and a selection of liqueurs, brandies, etc., as well as bottled and keg beer or lager, etc., not to mention all the usual spirits and minerals. It all starts to mount up. Not only is there the question of capitalisation but often an acute problem of storage which, in addition, must be very secure to satisfy the insurers and effective stock control. It is really a question of how far you want to go, or perhaps, can afford to go in terms of money and space consistent with the quantity and style of business being done.

The best advice is to start in a comparatively simple way, stocking those main items which are going to be asked for most frequently. One cannot for example stock a whole range of whiskies. Just offer two of the most popular; do the same for gin and so on. Keep the wine list as short as possible, carefully selecting a few good and reliable main types such as hock, red and white Bordeaux (sweet and medium), red and white Burgundy and perhaps a sparkling wine or two such as Champagne or a cheaper substitute. One can go on for ever but it is entirely a matter of policy. Do not, however, try to sell wines which are wrong for the type of trade being done. When selecting them ensure that by the time the mark up on cost is added they will not be overpriced in relation to the menu price structure. There is a tendency quite often to over-price wines. This leads to sales resistance and it is better to be content with a fair profit and move the stock than frighten people off.

A fair amount of assistance can be obtained from suppliers although today's trading conditions have caused a tightening up on hand-outs in various forms. It is however worth seeing what inducements any particular brewery or wine merchant will be prepared to offer. In some cases a bar may be fitted for example, but this sort of generosity would almost certainly mean a tie of some kind. Optics, which in themselves are com-paratively expensive items, could well be given as well as wine-cooling buckets, baskets, ash-trays and many other advertising pieces.

Whilst not so commonly practised now, it is worth seeing if a 'remote store' agreement can be arranged with a merchant or brewery. This in effect means that they will supply a stock, maintain it, stocktake periodically and make good stock sold. The items sold will then be charged for. Naturally the stock must be kept very securely and insured against loss. The obvious advantage to the restaurateur is that stock will not have to be paid for until sold, which avoids the capitalisation factor. It does, however, mean becoming tied to some extent and thereby losing the opportunity to buy competitively; it could also mean a narrower range to choose from.

Most breweries will be more than pleased to set up refriger-ated keg or larger installations free in order to obtain an outlet. Cooling trays for bottled beers too are sometimes available on a free loan basis, as well as sherry casks, etc. It is surprising what can be obtained when the breweries compete for your custom, so try them out.

Effect on Trade

There is little doubt that the granting of a licence will do much to enhance the business. It will invariably bring a better class of trade and particularly so in the evening. It increases turnover and profits, although the percentage is not as high as on food usually. It is difficult to contemplate party or function business without a liquor licence. As we have seen, people either go to a restaurant to eat out of necessity, or otherwise to spend a pleasant social evening, possibly celebrating some occasion. If the latter form of business it to be attracted, then a restaurant licence is a 'must'.

Just as a passing thought it should be mentioned that there is nothing to prevent a customer eating in an unlicensed place to give the waitress money to go to the 'pub' next door to fetch a drink to have with his meal. It must, however, be the customer's own money and cannot come out of the till or be put on the bill. If this practice were to be allowed to grow, however, then this particular caterer might just as well become licensed and have the profit.

Refreshment House Licence Act, 1969

Confusion is often experienced over the question of what constitutes and necessitates a 'Refreshment House Licence' in the operation of a restaurant or café. Not surprisingly, sometimes those contemplating the purchase of a catering business either imagine that they must hold a catering licence of some kind or that, since the term 'Refreshment House' is mentioned it must be to do with the sale of liquor. It is neither.

Under the Act, which had existed in a slightly different form for many years previously, any unlicensed café, or restaurant (i.e. not holding a liquor licence) that trades between the hours of 10.00 p.m. and 5.00 a.m. must apply to their local authority (Council) for a Refreshment House Licence. Sometimes late night disturbance can cause complaints from neighbours, or by virtue of the hours of trading, attract an undesirable element and thereby the attention of the police. In such cases the authority could withhold or withdraw the licence as it thought fit. It gives them control, although the authorities are not usually unreasonable or unsympathetic in bona fide cases, particularly with regard to cafés in markets, or transport undertakings. The authority can, therefore, fix the hours of trading and may fix a closing time not earlier than 11.00 p.m.

CHAPTER 14

Advertising the Business

How and to what extent to advertise the business always creates something of a quandary, for the costs of publicity can be heavy and sometimes the return very doubtful. There is little doubt in the author's mind that the most successful form of advertising is the one which costs nothing at all – the satisfied customer; there is nothing like personal recommendation by clients to their friends. Open a new business, hit the market right and then give the public what they want, particularly if it fills a gap in the local catering scene and your customers will quickly spread the gospel for you. Conversely, if the business is badly managed or trying to emulate a more successful competitor a few doors away, all the money spent on advertising will be wasted. The public will only come once. This fact apart then, how is it best to budget?

Budget

In Chapter 7 the question of overheads, and controlling them, was discussed. Expenditure on advertising can quickly snowball if not kept in check. It is really a question of what can be afforded, although any advertising agent will do his utmost to convince you that you cannot possibly afford not to. It is all a bit of a gamble really. When things are quiet it is natural to want to drum up trade and yet, because things are quiet, you

174

should be thinking twice about incurring expenditure, particularly on something which is intangible.

One has to be sensible and the best way to go about things is to plan a spread of publicity in the wisest possible way with a budget ceiling of £X per annum. This then becomes a budgeted overhead. Once the business becomes well established, expenditure on advertising becomes less necessary and then becomes a question of keeping the establishment's name in front of the public, or acquainting them with some newly planned feature or development.

Advertising Agents

In business one gets a fairly steady flow of 'reps' to deal with, trying hard to sell you something you can well do without. The most tenacious and persuasive form of representative is the advertising agent without a doubt. The tricks employed to get into the office are legion! Rarely do they announce their true identity but perhaps they say they are 'from the local hospital' when they are really trying to sell advertising space inside magazine covers. On other occasions they perhaps use the name of a local estate agent, when all they want is for you to advertise on a map of the area.

The biggest 'con' of all, which is now distinctly frowned on since it is 'unsolicited', is to send a proof through the post for a 'Trades Directory' with your establishment shown on a slip of paper ostensibly cut out of such a book. The 'proof' invariably gives the impression that it is a repeat and may say that unless alterations are requested the publishers will go to print or, worst of all, would the caterer please sign the proof as being correct. Such agencies rely on possible confusion, and the probability that the caterer will be under too much pressure to check it out. The practice is illegal under the Unsolicited Goods and Services Act but somehow still persists. The best way to treat these cases is to write 'not authorised' across it and send it back in an unstamped envelope.

Authorisation

For obvious reasons only one person, even if it is a husband

and wife partnership, should authorise advertising expenditure. This avoids duplication of thought and action and of such cases as referred to in the previous section. Under no circumstances should staff be allowed to take action, unless of course a manager has been given such authority.

Where to Advertise

To some extent the policy of publicising the business must be influenced by the geographical situation, the particular market that requires to be attracted and the timing of such advertising to be effective. It is perhaps unnecessary to comment on 'saturation' in the context of this book. Few caterers could afford it but the point is made.

If the business is in a resort, or a tourist centre, advertising in the town guide, particularly if party bookings are envisaged, is worthwhile. Visitors, especially those in bed and breakfast accommodation, like to know where they can eat. If the town should have a live publicity department and officer, quite a beneficial effect can be felt if full advantage is taken of whatever facilities are offered and a close liaison effected. Very often lists of places to stay at, or to eat in, are produced as small supplements to the guide and these are often distributed free to visitors who call at the town's publicity kiosk. Such lists often only give bald details of name and address, seating capacity and opening times, but it is worth being included. The advertisement in the main guide, however, should market the business well and stress particularly any features which are considered to have the edge on competitors.

Local Advertising

When a new extension, or perhaps a new kitchen even, has been completed it is something which will be good to advertise. In this connection a half page or page can be taken in the local news media with the support of all the caterer's contractors and normal trade suppliers, asociating themselves with the venture. This reduces the cost of advertising considerably since they will pay for their own spaces. The usual theme is to extend congratulations to the restaurant and express pleasure at being associated with the new works or whatever.

Depending on the geographical location of the business, i.e. whether it is out in the country or situated in the town, it is necessary to decide what the most beneficial media will be. The size and type of the market is of importance in this respect and where specifically the trade is going to come from. If in a country district, then clients will have to use their cars to come out and the area will be comparatively large. Therefore the county paper, if there is one, will be better spread than one in an isolated town unless, of course, there is only one isolated town to draw from.

In a town or city, particularly in a local situation, perhaps near a theatre or other entertainment, then the advertising should be aimed at this market if it is the intention to capture this kind of trade. An inducement such as a discount on production of the theatre programme is worth consideration. The programme type of advertising is perhaps better than on a 'safety curtain' as people tend to have forgotten the message by the time they come out. There is, however, a tendency to keep the programme. This type of advertisement too is easier to cancel and can be taken for shorter periods. The value of advertising on things such as the back of bus tickets is doubtful as people rarely look at them. One gets requests to advertise in the church magazine perhaps, but if you are running a night spot then it is hardly likely to be relevant.

Content

The advertisement should be bold and punchy and should *say* something. You are trying to sell your wares, so just inserting the name and address of the establishment is not enough. Gimmicky advertisements are all very well but they need to be very carefully and cleverly thought out or they can look foolish. A restaurateur acquaintance, somewhat exasperated at his lack of success and who has since sold, actually inserted an advertisement in the local press which stated that there was more than one restaurant in his particular street! No comment! If you think you are offering some special kind of service, then promote it hard. Do not hide it and lose it in the small print, but punch it out so that it catches the eye, stimulates immediate interest and is read first. If this effect is attained the reader will naturally want to know more, such as where or when, and all the relevant detail.

Logo

What is nowadays known as a 'logo', which is an identifying design particularly associated with the enterprise, is a good thing to have. It is a kind of trademark if you like. It gives style and promotes prestige, particularly if you write to clients a lot, offering quotations. It can be used on the headed notepaper and envelopes. It should not be difficult to design one which is appropriate, but be careful you do not infringe someone else's. Once designed it can be utilised in all newspaper advertisements and becomes identifiable in the public's mind with the establishment. Even a slogan could be used to good effect as long as it identifies.

Book Matches, etc.

Other sources of advertising are 'give aways' such as book matches, calendars, diaries, etc. All have their merit but are, of course, an expensive overhead which must be covered. It is largely a question of the style of business and class of client. Diaries and calendars tend to be rather overdone these days and in business one gets embarrassed with the number one receives. However, people who receive a surfeit usually give them to someone else and pass them on, so at least, in this respect, they are not totally lost or wasted.

Tent Cards, etc.

A well-designed 'tent card' placed on the table is often well received and it is surprising how many get taken away or are asked for. Clients eating for the first time, if they are suitably impressed, immediately want to tell their friends about their new 'find'. If they are able to pick up a card, whether it be of the tent type or not, this helps to promote the business and is very useful publicity and not quite so intangible as the results of newspaper or other advertisements. The restaurateur does, however, have to get the customer to the place first so that this is a form of supplementary advertising. There are always people who discover the establishment by accident though.

Television and National Advertising

Everyone knows and recognises the pull of television advertising, even on a regional basis, at peak viewing time. Buying a few seconds of time, however, is a very expensive business indeed to the average restaurant. Whilst it is true that a lot can be said in thirty seconds, unless one can afford to advertise at reasonably frequent intervals on a fairly continuous basis, I feel that one can do a very large amount of local newspaper advertising for much less cost and with greater return. Are people living fifty or one hundred miles away really likely to come to see you? The bread and butter is likely to come from a much more localised area. The same applies to any form of national advertising. It is never really worth considering for the small individual caterer. The expense would never justify the return.

Advertising the business requires very careful thought indeed. Know your market. Say something when you want to say it and say it in the right place at the right time, loud and clear. Nibbling away with bits and pieces in media which is not relevant to your market is a waste of time and money! Develop a recognisable marketing policy and budget for it.

CHAPTER 15

The Professional Approach

The Entrepreneur

An entrepreneur is described in one of the best works of reference as 'One who undertakes to start and conduct an enterprise or business, assuming full control and risk'. In this context, therefore, any small shopkeeper, café proprietor or restaurateur would be so classed. To me, however, whilst not disagreeing with the bald sense of the interpretation, an entrepreneur would be an individual businessman with above average flair, professional ability and instinct and with distinct emphasis on individuality. There is little doubt that the successful restaurateur will combine most or all of these qualities. As long as he is supported by first-class management, he need not be a 'professional' in the catering sense although, as has been remarked earlier in the book, there would be a distinct weakness in a small business if bereft of some craft skills.

It will be obvious from the foregoing chapters that there is a considerable amount of all-round knowledge needed to operate a catering establishment successfully. However, there is no reason why knowledge cannot be acquired and an effort made to increase one's professional ability in a particular field of weakness. Reading this book has probably alerted you to many of the problems and practicabilities which had not

180

crossed your mind before. Professionalism, in the business sense, is the opposite of amateurism. The fact that one is engaged in business to earn a living does not necessarily make one a professional, as an amateur approach could still be used. In the world of commerce, however, the amateur will rarely last long. How then can those with only basic knowledge succeed?

Self-Development

I started this book by recounting an experience of many years ago when I was told by the 'old man' that I would never finish learning. If we start with the realisation that we really all know very little, and just some more than others, then, with the right mental attitude and approach, embark on a policy of self-development, we are on the road to becoming a professional. It is, of course, easier to do this when one is young, but improving performance, particularly in business, is well within the reach of the more mature. Assuming that one already has reasonable business sense and acumen, and it is impossible to underline the importance of this too strongly, it afterwards becomes a question of application.

There is an abundance of reading material by specialists in their field on almost every subject connected with our industry. Whilst this book has covered a wide and, I hope, appropriate range of subjects, restrictions on space has meant only a basic approach based rather on a practical and common-sense level. No mention of the culinary art for example might be considered by some as a glaring omission. It would have been quite pointless as there are so many specialist books on the subject. A small word of advice here though: it is often better to buy those technical manuals chiefly intended for catering students rather than glossy examples intended for the housewife. The former are written by experts from the industry with a consequent commercial slant. A list of further recommended reading will be found in the appendix. A recent publication by the government-sponsored Small Firms Information Centre and written by Miles Quest, *Entering the Hotel and Catering Industry*, is worthwhile reading for the aspiring caterer. Also helpful, particularly for the young entrant, is *A Career in*

Hotels and Catering by John Fuller and David Gee. Many other useful booklets are also available.

Training Groups and Colleges

All small businesses in the industry are eligible to join the local Training Group of the Hotel and Catering Industry Training Board and are able to participate in seminars and short courses on a variety of subjects which foster efficiency. Telephone the Board (01 902 8865) and ask for the local Group Training Officer's address. The H.C.I.T.B. can give valuable assistance through their Small Business Services Agency. Write for their folder entitled *Small Business Services*.

The Trade Press

Taking the trade newspapers and magazines will help in keeping abreast with developments. Everyone takes a daily newspaper, watches television, or listens to the radio to keep up to date with all that is going on about them, or they might as well live on a desert island. Is it any less logical to cut oneself off from developments in the trade affecting one's livelihood? A surprising number do! It is very necessary to monitor progress and reports on the latest developments in new equipment, techniques, or convenience foods, but most of all, the constant changes in legislature that affects the running of the business. Having advance warning of possible changes in the law, or other matters, can sometimes be of considerable value in forward planning and thinking. Reading reports of what others in the industry are doing can be of benefit and stimulate one's own ideas which might be of use in developing an operation.

Trade Associations

The main trade association to which employers should belong is the British Hotels, Restaurants and Caterers Association (Telephone 01-499 6641). Formed out of a joining of the two main trade associations in 1972, this body acts for all sections of the industry. It is, if you like, the industry's watch-dog. As such, it makes representations to the government and its various departments on all matters of legislation which would affect the industry. It is similarly consulted by the Hotel and Catering Industry Training Board, all the various bodies concerned with tourism, the motoring organisations, and keeps a close eye on Parliamentary bills of a local nature which might constitute dangerous precedents.

The B.H.R.C.A., through its various specialist panels and committees, researches into all manner of things which are pertinent to any one sector of the industry and makes recommendations to its Board of Management and National Council. The regional divisions look after local matters affecting their members who are represented on the National Council. The Association also nominates representatives to other bodies such as the government's 'Little Neddy'. The Council and Board of Management represent a cross-section of the widest experience in the trade covering both small and large employers. In addition to all this it handles some 35,000 individual enquiries from its members each year on all kinds of problems affecting their businesses. There is an excellent corps of officers at headquarters who are well qualified and expert in specialised fields to deal with such matters.

In short, any forward-looking caterer cannot afford to be without the backing and services of such an organisation. Naturally is costs money to belong to it but the annual sub-scription is, after all, chargeable to tax and when this is taken into account is less than about fifty pence a week for the average member. This is a small price to pay for security and advice in addition to receiving a monthly magazine containing all the latest news and developments. It even offers the opportunity to advertise cheaply in a nationally distributed guide which has a separate restaurants section.

There are, of course, other trade bodies to which one can belong, such as the Restaurateurs Association of Great Britain, but none possesses the influence and power of the B.H.R.C.A. which represents the employers of the industry as a whole.

Other Associations

The Cookery and Food Association is a very old craft association which exists to ensure the perpetuation of the culinary art, and is open to employers and employees alike. It is also worth mentioning the industry's professional body, The Hotel, Catering and Institutional Management Association (H.C.I.M.A.) but it is scarcely pertinent to readers of this book, unless already a member, in which case you should already have the knowledge it contains! Membership of the H.C.I.M.A. is only possible through examination and whilst there is nothing to prevent anyone entering, the amount of preparation and study would be a very heavy commitment indeed. Correspondence courses leading to the examinations are available, however, if you are really keen.

Trade Exhibitions

A major exhibition of equipment by the manufacturers is now held in Birmingham alternating with Hotelympia in London where one can learn a lot about new equipment and food and drink lines as well as seeing cookery demonstrations and displays of the chef's art in the Salon Culinaire which, incidentally, has always been organised by the Cookery and Food Association. It is all instrumental in building up a store of knowledge and information, and a source of ideas and innovations that one can introduce into one's own operation.

Training Attitudes

Mention has already been made of the beneficial effects of training. The encouragement of youngsters by offering day-release to a local technical college is bound to affect their efficiency and introduce professionalism into the business. The patient and proper induction of new staff so that they are fully aware of their commitment pays dividends in the short as well as long term. The writing up of 'job descriptions' too in itself clears up many of the grey areas of responsibility and promotes efficiency. It is not suggested that small employers should go through all the avenues of 'identifying training needs' and finally producing training plans. It is not in context, nor would it be necessary, but a realisation that the efficiency of staff is linked with increasing profitability is appropriate. It is yet another facet of the more professional approach.

Further Reading

Bertram, Peter, *Fast Food Operations,* Barrie & Jenkins, 1975

Boella, M. J., *Personnel Management in the Hotel and Catering Industry,* Hutchinson, 1980

Bull, F. J. & Hooper, J. D. G., *Hotel and Catering Law,* Barrie & Jenkins, 1975

Combes, S., *Restaurant French,* Barrie & Jenkins, 1974

Combes, S., *Dictionary of Cuisine French,* Hutchinson, 1974

Fuller, J., *Modern Restaurant Service,* Hutchinson, 1982

Fuller, J. & Currie, A. J., *The Waiter,* Hutchinson, 1973

Fuller, J. & Gee, D. A. C., *A Career in Hotels and Catering,* Hutchinson, 1975

Gladwell, D. C., *Practical Maintenance and Equipment for Hoteliers, Caterers and Licensees,* Hutchinson, 1974

Kotas, Richard, *An Approach to Food Costing,* Hutchinson, 1973

Neil, Arthur, *Running Your Own Hotel,* Hutchinson, 1980

Small, M. R., *Catering for Functions,* Barrie & Jenkins, 1976

Quest, Miles, *Entering the Hotel and Catering Industry,* Small Firms Information Centre, Department of Industry, Abell House, John Inslip Street, London, SW1P 4LN, 1975